CLIMBING DOWN

How Leaders Descend To Their Destiny

BY
BRIAN ROTH

CLIMBING DOWN
How Leaders Descend to Their Destiny
By Brian Roth

1. BUS071000 2. BUS041000 3. BUS000000
Print ISBN: 978-1-949642-26-1
Ebook ISBN: 978-1-949642-27-8

Cover design by Jared Fite

All biblical references are taken from the
New American Standard Bible (NASB)

Printed in the United States of America

Authority Publishing
11230 Gold Express Dr. #310-413
Gold River, CA 95670
800-877-1097
www.AuthorityPublishing.com

CONTENTS

DEDICATION

Many people have shaped my life and steered me onto the road toward my destiny. To all those people, I say thank you. To my parents, Roger and Lou Roth, thanks for teaching me many things and allowing me the freedom to make many mistakes. Those mistakes helped to shape me. To my kids, Tyler, Tanyale, and T.J., thank you for being patient as I learned how to apply leadership and management in the family. To my siblings, Jon, Dawn, and Amy, you have always been supporters even when my ideas were crazy! Although we spent many years apart, Sharice and I always felt your love. To Carlos Seise and Tom Richards, mentors and superb leaders in their areas of gifting, thank you for listening to my ideas and keeping me focused. To John Hans and Jeff Zurcher, my brothers, thanks for using your gifts to co-labor with me in this and other ventures. John, you are a fantastic connector of people, and your connection to Jeff radically changed the course of this project. Jeff, you can write like no other! Thanks for accepting me as a brother and for the hours you spent taking the words I wrote and making them sensible and understandable. My 450 on the verbal part of the SAT didn't deter you from taking on this project, and I will always be grateful! To Darrin Fuller, whose gift I first saw with the crushed Mountain Dew can you drew in high school, thanks for sharing your gift in supporting this project!! To Jared Fite for your design guidance in helping to refine the images in this book and the book cover. To my King, Lord, and Savior, the God and creator of all things, may this book bring you glory because it is part of the reason you created me fifty-three years ago. Finally, to my wife, Sharice, thanks for loving me when I was not very lovable and for always being a warrior for causes I pursued. You are my BFF and my lover. You might be the only one that appreciates this, but this is for you baby!!

> Thanks for allowing me to be your hubby
> I'm better because of your light
> We may not always agree on things
> And maybe even have a fight
>
> But I wouldn't change our thirty-plus years
> Not a chance, oh no, no way
> I'm thankful you're my partner in crime
> So let me simply say
>
> I love you, baby, every day even more
> Waking up next to you makes me whole
> You are beautiful outside that's for sure
> And inside, an amazing soul

1

A NEW DIRECTION IN LEADERSHIP

Most people in organizations are conditioned to think like this: Climbing *up* is good; winners scrap and soar toward the pinnacle of achievement. Climbing *down* is bad; losers dwindle and drop toward the sewer of defeat.

So I'm encouraging you to climb down—naturally!

Why? Because conditioning is just that: conditioned thinking, not *correct* thinking.

And because **the less visible you become as a leader, the more valuable you become to your organization.** That is, visibility and value are inversely proportional.

Visibility is a measure of sight, how far one can see while driving or flying, for instance. Having a clear view of what's ahead is crucial, but if an organization's visibility is limited to how far out front a leader is, then the organization won't—can't—achieve more than the leader achieves.

In other words, when the organization looks out its front "windshield," can it see all the opportunities and challenges on the horizon, or can the organization only see the leader? In an organization filled with "look-at-me" leaders, people cannot see the horizon, the future.

Value is a measure of intrinsic worth someone assigns to an item, individual, or idea. Value, then, is not a fixed standard but rather a subjective evaluation, a perception. For instance, some may perceive a Babe Ruth rookie card to be worth $200,000, and others may perceive the card to be worth $20.

Leaders who link their organizational value to their organizational visibility limit their organizations' potential. Leaders who place their value to the organization on the visibility of *others*, however, augment their organizations' potential. These are leaders who climb down the leadership ladder and unlock the capacity of their constituents along the way, to the immense benefit of the organization.

Here's an illustration that addresses the inverse nature of visibility and value within the construct of leadership.

When our kids were younger and played sports, they and their teammates did not make a move without instruction—without the coach telling them something or the "coaches" (parents) in the bleachers yelling something. When they were older, playing high school sports, you might see one of the players talking to the team during a timeout or providing some instruction on the field. Players providing instruction to one another didn't reduce the value of the coach; rather, that occurrence increased the coach's value. Why? Because the coach's two eyes and ears might miss something, but having players who understand the coach's story (message) and know the direction in which they are to move without specific instructions demonstrates how valuable the coach has been in leading players to that point of confidence and maturity.

So…does a "reduced visibility" leader refrain from taking the podium at her company's annual meeting? Does he hide out in his office all day, with the door locked? Does she sit back and let others make all the decisions?

Absolutely not. Leaders who become less visible don't shirk responsibilities, cease to use their gifts, or avoid contact with others. But they do work to intentionally elevate followers so that they (the leaders) become harder to distinguish in a crowd… because followers "look like" leaders in aptitude, opportunity, confidence, and purpose.

Think of it this way: If a Ferrari were parked in a lot full of minivans, the Ferrari would be quite visible. But if a Ferrari were parked in a lot featuring other exotic sports cars, the Ferrari would be far less noticeable. Of course, regardless of where it was parked, the Ferrari retains the qualities that made it unique (and powerful!). But in the lot full of other exotic sports cars, that the car was a "Ferrari" would matter less because of the other high-end and powerful vehicles surrounding it.

So know that leaders who aspire to become less visible can be in the spotlight when helpful to their organization. But, more importantly, these leaders must want to be *behind* the spotlight, so they can point it at the organization's story and shine it on team members.

>> LEADERS WHO LINK THEIR ORGANIZATIONAL VALUE TO THEIR ORGANIZATIONAL VISIBILITY LIMIT THEIR ORGANIZATION'S POTENTIAL.

COMING ATTRACTIONS

Along with the inverse relationship between visibility and value, below are a few other key points from *Climbing Down*.

- Everyone can lead and manage.

- Leadership thinking impacts leadership behavior.

- Leadership and management are equally important, but different.

- There is a critical distinction between history, legacy, and destiny.

- Leaders get to choose their team, and followers get to choose who leads them.

- Employing a touchable and tangible leadership model will improve your leadership, whether you are a coach, teacher, executive, parent, pastor, legislator, etc.

I want to expound upon three of these points briefly.

First, you are endowed to lead, gifted with leadership ability. This ability is hardwired into you, into all humans. Sadly, many people fail to activate their leadership gift. Why? Because they don't believe they possess this gift, they don't know how to activate it, or they allow their circumstances to dominate them.

Let me explain it this way: When you purchase a new computer, it comes with pre-loaded software. The manufacturer of a computer installs software that allows the computer to function as designed. This software, however, is of no use unless it is activated, and computer users often need a unique key to unlock the software to experience the full benefit of it. The same is true regarding our capacity to lead. We are "manufactured" with the gift of—the potential for—leadership. This leadership "software" resides on the hard drive of our being, but we often lack the key to unlock it, which prevents us from delivering the full benefit of our leadership gift to others.

Does the above software metaphor apply to you? If so, take heart, because the leadership ladder is a key that will help you unlock and apply your leadership potential.

Second, our thinking drives our behavior. Of course, there are plenty of empirical studies to support that claim, but most of us would agree with that statement based on our experience alone. Thinking is at the center of everything we do. Wrong thinking often results in undesirable outcomes, and right thinking frequently produces positive results. Thus, how we think is critically important to how we live our lives, to the impact we have on those around us, and to our leadership.

Because thinking drives behavior, your leadership potential is inseparable from how you think. For instance, if you *don't* believe you have the ability to lead, you're right (even though your thinking is incorrect), and if you *do* think you have the ability to lead, you're right. So, to fully realize your leadership potential, make sure your thinking is—and remains—renewed.

Third, to make leadership touchable and tangible, leaders must take philosophy and turn it into application. For example, knowing that "vision" is part of effective leadership is helpful, but communicating a vision so that it connects with people and moves an organization forward is essential. Likewise, knowing that empowering people is critical toward achieving a vision is useful for leaders, but only by actually empowering people will leaders help their organizations arrive at the destination described by their vision.

THE LEADERSHIP LADDER

The *Climbing Down* leadership model is represented by a ladder (Figure 1.1). The remainder of this chapter will touch on the various aspects of this model, and the second half of the book will explore the model in detail.

In several of his works, John Maxwell discusses five stages, or levels, of leadership: *position, permission, production, people development,* and *pinnacle.* Maxwell's principles were the catalyst behind reshaping my views on leadership, compelling me to improve how I led within the navy and within my family. Of course, Maxwell's views on leadership are also reflected in the leadership ladder.

There is a critical difference, however, in how Maxwell and I conceptualize leadership. In Maxwell's five-stage model, leaders are assumed to climb up, toward the *pinnacle,* the peak, the highest level. Conversely, with the leadership ladder, I encourage leaders to climb down toward *personhood,* the bedrock level of leadership. I'm persuaded that *down* is the better direction for leaders to go because climbing up (away from others) seems counter to what I've seen from great leaders...whose presence in the trenches provides real inspiration for the people around them.

Additionally, the leadership ladder model provides clear incentives for improving one's leadership, noting *why* a leader should want to move down to the next leadership stage (to gain followers, to make history, to build a legacy, and to reach destiny).

I believe that listing the expected result of effective leadership at a particular stage can compel leaders to act in such a way as to achieve that result. That is, I intend to convince people to *do* leadership better...not merely to understand it better.

So please understand that I am not trying to reinvent the wheel...er, the ladder. No, I don't deserve credit for developing original principles; instead, what I have done herein is to restructure—to enhance, perhaps—some ideas that have helped me, and I've clarified these ideas to benefit you...so that you can apply them today, wherever you are on your leadership journey.

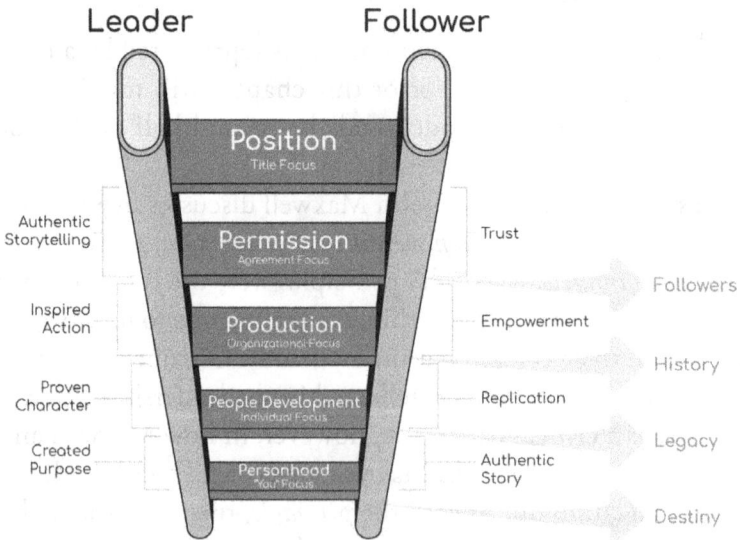

Leader   **Follower**

Position
Title Focus

Authentic Storytelling   Permission   Trust
Agreement Focus

Inspired Action   Production   Empowerment   Followers
Organizational Focus

Proven Character   People Development   Replication   History
Individual Focus

Created Purpose   Personhood   Authentic Story   Legacy
"You" Focus

Destiny

Figure 1.1 – The Leadership Ladder

RUNGS AND RAILS

Just like with an actual ladder, rungs and rails are the essential pieces of the leadership ladder. The ladder's **rungs** represent the five stages of leadership, and the ladder's rails represent the actions necessary to move from one rung to the next.

Mirroring John Maxwell's five levels of leadership, the five rungs of the leadership ladder are:

- *Position* – People follow you because they have to.

- *Permission* – People follow you within an agreed upon boundary.

- *Production* – People follow because of the impact you have on the organization.

- *People Development* – People follow you because of the impact on them.

- *Personhood* (Maxwell's original label for his fifth level; he now calls it *Pinnacle*) – People follow you because of who you have become.

As you can see by looking at the leadership ladder, the *positional* rung is the widest, and there are several reasons for this, including (a) everyone starts on this rung, (b) many people lack the knowledge required to move off this rung, and (c) our actions sometimes move us back to this rung after we start to climb down. The last of these reasons begs the question, "Why would a leader regress, or move back, to the positional rung after leaving it?" Short answer: The leader breaks the followers' trust; hence, the leader loses permission to lead the followers and regresses up the ladder to the *position* rung.

Conversely, the *personhood* rung is the narrowest rung—because climbing down the ladder is difficult. You must climb down one rung at a time, after all. Consequently, to reach the *personhood* rung, you first must progress along each of the other rungs, with each rung requiring much effort and investment, from not only leaders but also followers. Reaching the *personhood* rung may require an entire lifetime of effort and investment.

The **rails** on the *Climbing Down* leadership ladder represent how one moves from one rung, or stage, to the next. For movement to occur, the leader must take action, and the follower must initiate corresponding (re)action. Remember, followers get to choose who leads them, so their reactions are not a given.

On the leader's rail, the following actions are required.

- *Authentic storytelling* is a picture of the future that is better than the present reality told with originality. It is the combination of mission and vision.

- *Inspired actions* are actions that derive their energy from the authentic story—from thinking about talking about the story regularly.

- *Proven character* is the fixed, unchangeable portion of our character that establishes standards for what is acceptable conduct and what is not.

- *Created purpose* is the original intent for you and your organization. Questions that uncover created purpose include "Why was this organization started?" and "Why are you here in this time and this place?"

On the follower's rail, the following actions are required.

- *Trust* in a leader, that a leader has created a safe space where a follower can freely bring ideas, experiences, innovations, and creativity.

- *Accepting empowerment* from a leader, with empowerment being the authority, knowledge, skills, and attitude required to complete an assignment.

- *Replication* of the outward actions, words, and behaviors of a leader.

- *Authentic story* is the follower's mission and vision that is (a) aligned with the organization's story and (b) told to others in the organization.

When leaders and followers both take action on a particular level of the leadership ladder, the following positive **outcomes** occur.

- *Followers (permission* rung) – A willing follower is one who accepts the purpose and the related story of a leader; achieving the *followers'* milestone occurs when a follower trusts a leader.

- *History (production* rung) – History is an event or sequence of events bound by time; achieving the *history* milestone occurs when a leader takes inspired actions and a follower accepts the empowerment offered by a leader.

- *Legacy (people development* rung) – Legacy is one person's story that is carried forward by others; achieving the *legacy* milestone occurs when (a) a leader's character is proven to a follower and (b) a follower starts to replicate a leader by functioning in a similar manner to the leader.

- *Destiny (personhood* rung) – Destiny is arriving at the location described by the organization's story and guarded by the organization's purpose. Reaching the *destiny* milestone occurs when the created purpose of the organization intersects with the authentic stories of followers.

CHEESE BALLS...OR MONKEY BARS?

The main challenge of accurately identifying the components of a construct as robust as leadership concerns the lens through which one views leadership. (In this instance, "lens" means *worldview*, one's outlook on life framed by experiences and beliefs.)

For example, your idea of *proven character* might be different than mine. You might say someone with proven character is someone who has integrity. I might agree, but your idea of integrity might be "honesty," and mine might be the "completeness or wholeness of words and actions." Now, those definitions of integrity aren't necessarily opposing, yet even a minor difference in meaning can be enough to alter the lens through which we understand or view something over time.

The game of telephone is an excellent example of how little variances can make significant differences. In case you did not play that game as a youngster, here's how it works.

Players sit in a circle, and the "operator" starts the game by whispering—one time only—a phrase into the ear of the person to one side of him/her. From there, the phrase is passed around the circle in the same way (a one-time whisper) until it reaches the person on the other side of the operator. That person announces the phrase to the group, and then the operator announces his/her initial phrase. The difference in the first-whispered and last-whispered phrases typically is substantial and produces good laughs all around.

In this game, each person generally hears and understands the phrase a little differently—and thus shares it a little differently than the previous person. Hence, as the phrase is passed around the circle, slight differences build into a big difference. For instance, the initial phrase may be, "The moon looks like a cheese ball," and the final phrase may be, "The zoo has monkey bars."

Or, perhaps the experience of going to the eye doctor may resonate better with you. When you have your vision checked, you look through a device and answer questions such as, "What's better: one or two? What's better: three or four?" Initially, there does not seem to be much difference between lenses one and two (or three and four). However, when the optometrist asks you to read the smallest line on the chart, the minor differences in lenses can be enough to make the line clear—or not.

Bottom line: We interpret constructs and ideas differently—even if only slightly—because our worldviews differ. How, then, can we reconcile these differences? (This is a critical question, as slight differences in how we see the world can significantly alter the interpretation of what we communicate.)

In this book, I will attempt to cut through possible differences in interpretation by utilizing the original meaning of the term I'm discussing. Using this approach should put us on common ground, regardless of worldview.

For example, when discussing *character*, I will go to the origin of the term or the original usage word—and I'll address the idea from that basis. Doing this will allow us to recognize that *character* comes from the idea of "etched in stone or of a statue, something that is fixed, permanent, and immovable regardless of the environment."

Although I would be naive to think everyone who reads this will agree with all that I say, I do hope that, by using this word-origin (etymology) approach, we can have a meaningful discussion in which we are speaking the same language... allowing us to agree in the end, that, yes, "the moon looks like a cheese ball."

FINAL THOUGHTS

The title of this book may strike you as odd—because we are conditioned to believe that climbing *up* the ladder is required for us to be successful. But I think that the most effective way to ensure success within an organization is to climb down the leadership ladder. I am convinced that the less visible leaders are within their organizations, the more valuable leaders are to their organizations...just like the most valuable part of a tree is its roots.

According to Simon Sinek, "There are leaders, and there are those that lead. Leaders hold a position of power or influence. Those who lead inspire us."[1] Building on Sinek's statement, true leaders are obsessed with a purpose—not power—and inspire action—not adoration—in those around them. Consequently, if you want to be powerful or adored, leadership is not the business for you, because you are motivated to climb up the corporate ladder...*away* from others.

However, if you are motivated by purpose, you are committed to climbing *toward* others, down the leadership ladder.

Which way are you climbing? And what about the "great leaders" whom you have encountered over the years...as far as you can tell, which way were they climbing?

My objectives with this book are (a) to challenge how you think about leadership and (b) to provide a framework that will allow you to improve your leadership, regardless of what point you may be in your journey. And my hope is that this book will be the beginning of transformation within and through you!

2

LEADING AND MANAGING:
Honey, What Did You Get Done This Week?

As I walked through the door at the end of another week, my beautiful wife, Sharice, greeted me with these words, "Honey, what did you get done this week?"

Now, a question such as "What did you accomplish?" seems like a very straightforward one. The perspectives from which that question was asked and answered can be a problem, however. If those perspectives differ, the answer to a simple question becomes much more complicated than necessary.

Our conversation on that evening continued something like this:

> Me: "We talked about changing the organization's structure slightly—not because the organizational structure will solve problems but because it often either inhibits or promotes growth."
>
> Her: "So, did you change the structure?"
>
> Me: "No, we talked about what changing the structure *might* look like and how that could positively influence the organization."
>
> Her: "Oh, great. So, then what did you get done this week?"
>
> Me: "We spent some time looking at what other differentiators we might be able to introduce into the marketplace

to position ourselves to become the provider of choice in our business."

Her: "Oh, great. So, are you the provider of choice?"

Me: "No, we are putting things in place today that will hopefully get us there in the future."

Her: "Oh, great. So, what did you get done this week?"

Now, I may not be the sharpest knife in the drawer, but I could see that we were failing at executing a fundamental skill necessary in any marriage: We were failing to communicate even though we were having a conversation.

Hence, I eventually decided to take this communication challenge head-on. So, I said to my wife, with overdue brilliance, "I don't understand your question."

For some reason we humans, when we get puzzled about something, often tilt our heads sideways as if our brains are hurting and too heavy for our necks. That's what my wife did when I told her I didn't understand her "What did you get done this week?" inquiry; so I knew she was confused by my inability to answer a seemingly simple question. After all, she did not ask me to enlighten her on the meaning of life—she just wanted me to tell her what I did at work that week!

After her head returned to a perfectly upright position, she rephrased her question as, "What did you check off your list?"

There...that was it—the heart of her question revealed. The light bulb blazed inside my head. Not the cheap, twenty-watt incandescent filament type, mind you. But rather, an LED directional floodlight. Sharice was not asking a general question about my week but rather a very specific one: What *management* activities did I complete this week? The disconnect between us stemmed from my providing a *leadership* answer to a management question. The reason we could not effectively resolve a fundamental question pertained to the fact that we were speaking different languages.

Different Is Good

The difference between leadership and management was freshly presented to me by Bill Weisbrod. Bill was my boss when our organization was struggling to find its way forward. Bill framed our problems as *tactical* and *strategic*, and he stressed how tactical activities (managing) would dominate strategic thinking (leading) unless we committed ourselves to dedicate time to thinking strategically.

Failing to recognize the difference between leadership and management—and thus becoming bogged down in management tasks—is commonplace and lies at the heart of why many people and organizations do not reach their maximum capacity, why they are unable to transform the potential energy contained in their leadership ability into kinetic energy visible in leadership action.

Why do people seem unable to distinguish between leadership and management?

Perhaps because nearly all people perform both management and leadership functions daily.

Or, perhaps because people overcomplicate both management and leadership and thus fail to see a simple way that the phenomena are fundamentally different.

For instance…

You might decide to sell your house and purchase a motor home to allow your family to obtain a different perspective. Or your company might choose to scrap an entire product line due to eroding margins. These are leadership decisions because they involve significant *change.*

Instead of a change in your lifestyle, you might decide to remodel your house or to build an addition to increase the square footage of your living space. Or, your company may choose to continue with its current product line but implement automation toward augmenting margins. These are management functions because they involve *improvement.*

Leadership is about turning the ship onto the desired course, whereas management is operating the ship so that it moves along that course efficiently. If you (a) merely turn the ship onto the desired course but can't operate the ship well or (b) can operate the ship well but can't get it on the right course, you will not be pleased with your result. In this, we can recognize that leadership and management are equally important.

The challenge we face is *how do we evaluate whether we should lead or manage?* To solve this, we need to ask ourselves—regularly—the following questions:

- Am I leading, and should I be?

- Am I managing, and should I be?

This approach may seem simplistic, but that's the beauty of it: Frequently asking yourself these simple questions will force you to pause and consider the concepts of change (leadership) and improvement (management). And so that you can better understand *how* leadership and management differ, we will spend some time defining each phenomenon, starting with leadership.

>> LEADERSHIP IS ABOUT TURNING THE SHIP ONTO THE DESIRED COURSE WHILE MANAGEMENT IS OPERATING THE SHIP SO THAT IT MOVES ALONG THAT COURSE EFFICIENTLY.

LEADERSHIP DEFINED

The definition of leadership is…varied. For instance, John Maxwell, Peter Drucker, and Myles Munroe, three respected leadership thinkers, each conceptualize leadership differently. For Maxwell, "The true measure of leadership is influence, nothing more or nothing less."[1] Drucker states, "Leadership is not magnetic personality, that can just as well be a glib tongue. It is not 'making friends and influencing people,' that is flattery. Leadership is lifting a person's vision to higher sights, the raising of a person's performance to a higher standard, the building of a personality beyond its normal limitations."[2] And Munroe identifies leadership as "others' willful submission of their authority to yours."[3]

Each of these definitions is valid—and useful. For this book, however, I will use this definition:

> **Leadership is (a) telling an authentic story that facilitates others' trust in you; (b) taking inspired actions that empower others to become active participants in the story; (c) being driven by proven character that bears fruit replicated in others; and (d) connecting with your created purpose and connecting others with theirs.**

This definition contains four components of leadership that I believe are sequential and circular—*sequential* because you cannot empower people who don't trust you and *circular* because you cannot tell an authentic story if you don't have an idea where the story ends. The sequential-and-circular aspect of leadership is what makes leading so...difficult: People want to become better leaders but don't know where to start. Consequently, many leaders become frustrated and feel unsure about how to move forward. My hope, however, is that this book both alleviates frustration and makes a path forward for leaders.

Let's look in-depth at the first component: *telling an authentic story that facilitates others' trust in you.* (Note: Although authentic storytelling is the first facet, the first *rail*, of the leadership ladder, it is not more important than the other rails. Taking inspired actions built upon proven character and understanding your reason for existence, both personally and organizationally, are also necessary if you truly desire to be a leader who transcends the "normal" quality of leadership that we observe around us today.)

We can all remember when, as kids, we asked our parents to tell us a story. Why? Because stories take us out of our present reality and place us within a better future. In other words, stories allow us to see ourselves within a different place or time even though we realize that we aren't actually "there."

When our parents told us stories authentically—as if they too *believed* the story—we were captivated. Do you remember those days? More importantly, can you build upon those days? I ask that because the ability to tell an authentic story is a necessary skill for any leader.

The Story of Mission and Vision

Myles Munroe views mission as a general assignment for an individual or organization and vision as a specific/unique assignment for an individual or organization. Webster's Dictionary defines *mission* as "a specific task performed by a group or individual" and *vision* as a "dream" or "imagination." Considering how these two sources define mission and vision, the two terms seem to be different…and interchangeable. That these two terms are used both similarly and differently depending upon the context could be confusing—and irrelevant.

Here's what I mean: The key point isn't whether you choose to use mission or vision…or, like me, if you combine those words into one term: "story." Rather, what is important is *where* this mission/vision/story resides.

If your mission/vision/story (let's use "MVS," for short) only hangs in the executive hallway and only shows up in the annual report, which label you use—whether "mission," "vision," or "story," is irrelevant. Why? Because those words are nothing more than that: words. Lip service. Empty.

The value in the MVS is when these words go to work. With everyone. Everyday. When the MVS is alive, purpose permeates all levels of the organization. As a result, all employees—no matter how long they have been in the organization—can connect their jobs with the bigger picture. When this happens, the MVS has the impact it is intended to have.

My experience is that most employees incorrectly view the MVS as a statement that is important for the corporate office only, and hence the MVS is not something the typical employee needs to understand...especially the further an employee is removed from the corporate office.

But things can—and do—change within an organization when a leader begins authentically telling the organization's story. As noted above, I view *story* as a combination of mission and vision, and authentic storytelling is presenting an original-yet-realistic picture of the future that is better than the present reality. This authentic story allows employees to see themselves, their coworkers, and their families in a place where they have not yet been but where they would certainly like to go.

All that said—with MVS—please know that I am not attempting to jettison "mission" and "vision" from organizational vernacular. *Vision* is quite useful, actually, in helping us understand the difference in leadership and management.

>> THE VALUE IN THE MISSION / VISION / STORY IS
WHEN THESE WORDS GO TO WORK.

LET ME "PUTT" IT THIS WAY

Vision differs from *sight*. Vision is a picture of what could exist in the future, whereas sight is a picture of what exists now. Vision pertains to leadership, in that leaders must look to the future of the organization to deliver change; sight pertains to management, in that managers must see the present reality of the organization to deliver improvement.

To further drive my point home, shaping a proper vision (foresight) normally requires clear sight (insight) regarding current conditions. The game of golf illustrates this.

In golf, the best putters visualize—create a vision for—the putt before they step up to the ball. They do this, in part, by using insight: They observe the direction of the grass along with the slope and the undulations of the green to develop a picture that results in the ball dropping into the cup. Watching these putters before they strike the ball, we begin to see their vision for the putt, which is revealed by how they position their feet, the force of their practice swings, and the line painted by their eyes on the green. When the ball is struck and begins rolling toward the cup, their vision turns into sight—and we see whether their vision is realized (if they make the putt).

Of course, making a putt, though often difficult, especially given the high-pressure stakes of professional golf, is not as complex as leading a team or organization. For example, in professional golf, by rule only two people, the golfer, and his/her caddie are allowed any input regarding the vision for a putt—hence only two people need to "buy into" that vision. (And if the golfer and caddie disagree on the vision for the putt, then only one person, the golfer, needs to buy into the vision.) For organizational success, however, tens, hundreds, or even thousands of people need to buy into a vision. So how does a leader influence others to embrace that yet-tangible picture of a future state when that picture isn't their own?

Through authentic storytelling.

While a vision statement may be a useful way for an employee's brain to connect with the organization, an authentic story is a much better way for an employee's heart to connect with the organization. Why? Because we grew up on stories (not on vision statements)!

Often, we read a novel and have a pretty good idea how it is going to end...even without knowing all the details of the plot. And sometimes we can even see how the author might have gone a different direction while still arriving at the same ending.

Organizational stories are no different. Often, the end of the story is understood—the destination where the organization wants to arrive is known—without employees knowing all the details concerning how the organization will get there. Herein, we see the importance of and connection between leadership and management.

Authentic storytelling is a leadership function; the leader must describe the destination at which the organization will arrive. Filling in the details along the journey—writing the chapters of the book, if you will—is a management function. Both functions must work together. If an organization doesn't know the end of its journey (leadership failure), the content of the chapters lacks purpose and potency, and chapters may as well not be written. And if the chapters are not written well (management failure), then the plot will never be completed.

In short: Leaders share a story that managers write; leaders describe a picture that managers paint; leaders see the invisible that managers make visible. If leaders and managers don't work together, the organization will either be very small or very poorly operated.

MANAGEMENT DEFINED

As has been stated, management is equally important but different from leadership. In a business context, managers are critical in providing and shaping the processes and administration that allow the organization to move forward, gaining ground toward its desired destination. In other words:

> *Management is creating a framework that enables progress within an existing story.*

To build this framework, managers find (a) a character within the leader's authentic story they can identify with or (b) a chapter in which they can craft details that will cause the book to start to take shape. Sometimes, the leader needs to help connect a manager with his/her character or point him/her to the chapter for which the manager might have the most impact. But, ultimately, the manager must embrace that character or chapter—must *own* the final version of that character or chapter—for the organization's story to be completed.

The conclusion of the story, the destination, always needs to be at the forefront. The conclusion must be part of all conversations, so that the different characters come together cohesively and so that each chapter fits together, building toward the desired destination. When the conclusion becomes gray or falls from an organization's daily thinking and conversation, managers will start to write their own story and fight for their story to overrule others' stories. Competing stories result in an organization that works hard but doesn't go anywhere. I refer to this phenomenon as *the treadmill effect* because the organization is running hard but not seeing a change in scenery.

Perhaps the following example will tie this together.

My last organization needed a new and authentic story, so they hired me to develop one. The ending to that new story—the new destination for our company—was delivering a superior customer experience. That was the destination I set (setting it was leadership function). However, I didn't create the framework or the processes and systems to get us to that destination; rather, the managers working for me did that. They determined the seven areas of focus and developed the practices to ensure we remained on the road to superior customer experience.

REAL LIFE MISAPPLICATION

Please know that confusing leadership and management is not a phenomenon unique to business or to business people.

In football, for instance, many incorrectly apply the concepts of leadership and management. During the broadcast of a football game, one often hears the announcers say that the quarterback is the on-field *leader*. If you subscribe to my definition, being labeled a "leader" would imply that the quarterback is creating and communicating an authentic story for his team and inspiring teammates to reach the destination described by that story. However, in all the years I played football, not one of my coaches expected the quarterback to develop his "own" story; instead, developing the story and articulating it with authenticity was the responsibility of the head coach and his offensive and defensive coordinators. The quarterback's role, then, is to *manage* the game, writing the chapters of the story laid out by the coaches during practice that week. Said another way, the coaches write the story and the quarterback is necessary to manage the flow, the process of the game to allow the story to reach its intended ending: victory.

If the quarterback writes his own story during the game, then (a) either the coaches are unnecessary, (b) the coaches did a poor job of conveying the story, or (c) the quarterback is operating independently. If any of these is true, the story likely will not reach its intended ending week after week.

If football's not your thing, let me try a different example: education. Within this context, our educational system would be better served if teachers were permitted to be *leaders* in the classroom—permitted to create a story for their students and then inspire them to move toward that story's destination. The reality is, though, that teachers are classroom *managers*; they develop a framework to ensure that someone else's story is consistently realized. Often, and sadly, "someone else's" story for the classroom is merely that all the kids must pass the standardized test so that the school continues to receive government funding. That is not a very inspiring story for teachers or students!

I am not saying that the above is the right story for our educational system. But ask teachers today, and they will tell you they manage the curriculum each day to ensure the story for their school concludes as intended: with good scores on the standardized tests, pay raises for staff, and future funding for the school.

I could continue with example after example of where we say "leadership," but we mean "management." Again, I am not saying leadership is more important than management, but I am saying that leadership and management are different...and that understanding this difference and creating a balance between leadership/management is critical to maximizing personal and organizational effectiveness.

Think of it this way: If you use a butter knife to eat your peas, you might eventually accomplish what you set out to do, but you will have a harder time accomplishing your goal than if you use a spoon. Choosing the correct tool for the task is critical to accomplish the task effectively. Leadership and management are distinct tools. If we continue to manage when we should lead, or to lead when we should manage, there will be many peas on the floor!

WHEN TO LEAD AND WHEN TO MANAGE

As stated earlier, we need to ask, "When should we lead, and when should we manage?" Asking ourselves that question is important, but knowing how to answer it is even more important.

Keep in mind that our default mode is to manage (and I'll discuss why in the next chapter). So, an efficient way to understand whether we should lead or manage is to gain an understanding of when to lead. Here are some questions to help with that understanding.

- Does your organization understand the story?

- Is the story believed to be authentic?

- Can others tell the story effectively?

- Is your organization focused on discipline and motivation, or is your organization inspired?

- Will the current path your organization is traveling result in arriving at the desired destination?

- When you sit in a meeting, are ideas flowing freely? Is there vetting of different ideas?

- Can you remember the last time the organization implemented something that wasn't its original idea?

- Would the organization make progress if you took a sabbatical for a month?

- Does your organization have a high rate of employee retention?

These types of questions give you a quick peek behind the curtain regarding how effective your leadership has been. If the answer to these or similar questions is "no," then you need to consider leading more.

FINAL THOUGHTS

Leadership and management are different but equally important, in the same way that pointing a ship in the right direction (leading) is equally as important as driving the ship well (management). Effective organizations are comprised of individuals who know how to properly balance leadership and management. When balanced properly, leadership and management function together in a way that both inspires and empowers people to achieve what previously seemed unattainable.

You've heard the quotes that go something like this: "If you can't measure it, you can't change it," or "If you can't measure it, you can't improve it." Those sayings certainly are true from a management perspective but not from leadership perspective.

Leadership is hard to measure, but that doesn't mean we shouldn't be leading. How effective is your MVS? That's tough to tangibly assess, but that doesn't mean MVS shouldn't be woven into the organization. Trust can be tough to quantify, but that doesn't mean we can't improve it. Proven character is subjective in some respects, but that doesn't mean you can't change it. We have to learn how to separate our leadership thinking from our management thinking in order to improve each, because how we improve or change them is different.

3

BALANCING ACT(ION)

The previous chapter introduced leadership and management as two different-but-equally-important concepts. Let me reaffirm that: Leadership and management *are* different but equally important. And to quote Bon Jovi, "Hold on. I'm not done. One more time…with feelin!"[1]—leaders are not more important to an organization than managers; both roles are equally important.

Now, the statement "equally important" doesn't mean that the organization must be comprised of 50% leaders and 50% managers. Instead, what I mean by *equally important* is "balanced"—you need the proper amount of leadership working with (balanced against) the proper amount of management.

Remember the simple equation from high school physics: $W1*D1 = W2*D2$, with *w* representing weight and *d* representing distance? This equation indicates that you can balance two different weights if the distances between the weights and the fulcrum are different, as shown in the second scale in Figure 3.1. (Did I mention my father was a physics professor and that I have a physics degree?)

>> LEADERSHIP AND MANAGEMENT ARE EQUALLY IMPORTANT BUT DIFFERENT, MEANING THEY SHOULD BE BALANCED.

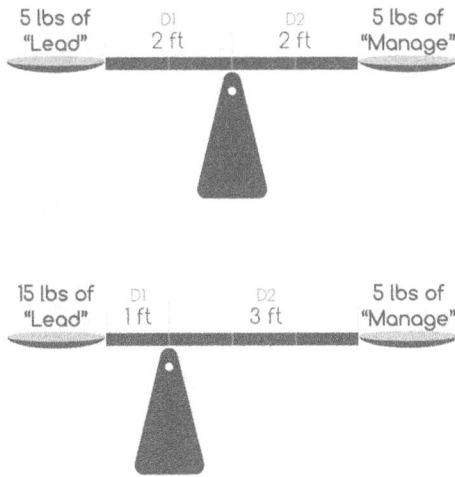

Figure 3.1 – Balanced Leadership and Management

To further demonstrate how leadership and management interface within organizations, I've developed—with Dr. Jeff Zurcher and Jared Fite—some diagrams. These graphics attempt to illustrate that:

- Balancing leadership and management enables people to contribute in their areas of skill.

- Without balance, ample attention will not be given to some leadership or management functions.

- Imbalance results in constraints that limit the potential of the organization due to the limited attention that is given to some management and leadership functions.

Figure 3.2 shows the relationship between leadership and management, and how the percentage of time spent managing and leading can change as one moves through different roles in an organization. This diagram assumes that an individual can give only 100% to leading, managing, or some combination of the two. For example, if one is leading 75% of the time, one can only manage 25% of the time. I'm not insinuating that the percentages of time leading and managing are equal every day. Rather, I'm simply asserting that every day one spends some amount of time managing and some leading—and that properly balancing leadership and management is critical within our own lives, within our families, and within our organizations.

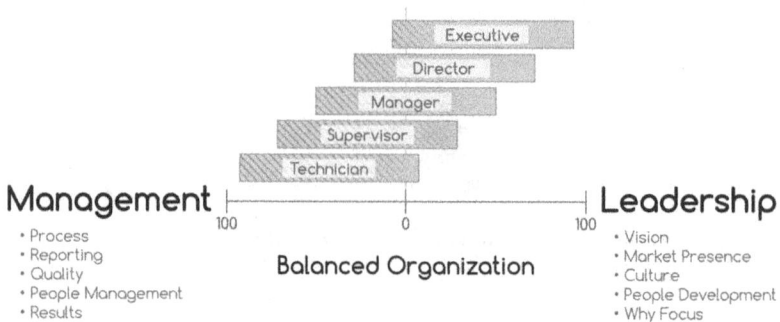

Figure 3.2 – Balanced Organization

When leadership and management are balanced, organizations function effectively and can achieve and sustain superior results. Why?

Because people are allowed the freedom to work closer to their maximum capability in (balanced) organizations that put equal weight on leadership and management functions. Operating toward their maximum capability helps employees to see their significance—resulting in a more productive workforce. A more productive workforce has a greater probability of producing consistent and sustainable results.

By the way, you can change the titles on this diagram from a *technician, director, etc.* to *father, mother,* and *children* and apply this concept to your family; for a church, you can use *pastor, staff, deacons,* and *congregation.* The point is that regardless of the organization, this diagram shows the balanced relationship between leadership and management that is necessary for a healthy organization, regardless of why the organization exists. I am defining *health* in this case to mean "more engaged and empowered" parishioners, family members, etc., and a healthy organization has an environment conducive to higher performance, service, relationships, and so on.

LOSS OF BALANCE

Now, let's contrast the balanced organization with one that is unbalanced. Many of us have been around people who are called "micro-managers" or may have been employed by organizations in which the bosses seemed to be more interested in doing your job than in doing theirs. Likewise, you may have had (or still have!) parents who try to make all your decisions—even after you've reached adulthood. Or, you may have been on a sports team wherein the assistant coaches were not allowed to assist. These are examples of organizations that are unbalanced—over-managed and under-led (Figure 3.3).

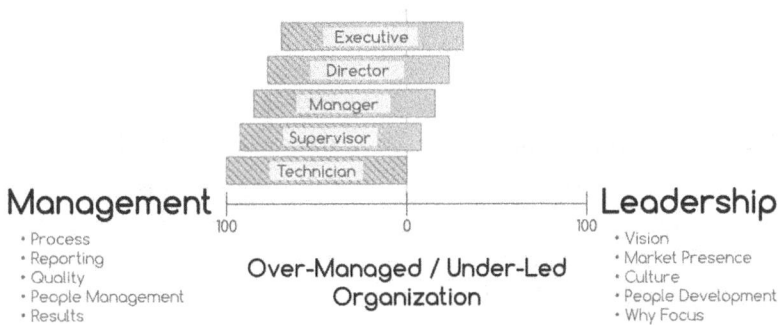

Figure 3.3 – The Over-Managed / Under-Led Organization

You might use an app called Snapchat or might have read about the challenges within Uber. These organizations were started by people with unique ideas. They had great vision and could see the potential impact on society. However, these organizations have at times struggled mightily to figure out how to implement process and procedures, making them examples of organizations that are unbalanced—over-led and under-managed (Figure 3.4).

29

		Executive		
		Director		
		Manager		
		Supervisor		
		Technician		

Management ├──────────────┼──────────────┤ **Leadership**

100   0   100

Management	Over-Led / Under-Managed Organization	Leadership
• Process		• Vision
• Reporting		• Market Presence
• Quality		• Culture
• People Management		• People Development
• Results		• Why Focus

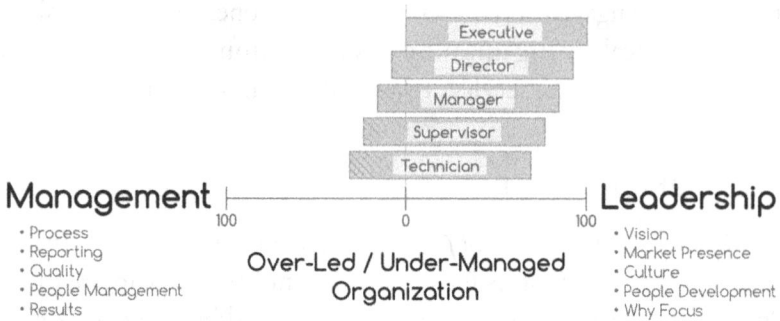

Figure 3.4 – The Over-Led / Under-Managed Organization

Is an unbalanced organization a bad organization? After all, there is plenty of evidence that shows these organizations are profitable and provide adequate products or services. So, are unbalanced organizations a problem?

Yes, because persons in unbalanced organizations do not achieve their potential—and therefore, neither does the organization. What makes organizations great is not benchmarking against average companies, because we can always find organizations (or families) that seem more dysfunctional than ours…but what value does measuring our performance against theirs provide? That is, measuring ourselves against mediocrity may make us feel better for a while, but, in the end, such a measurement is uninspiring and not motivating. In my opinion, comparing our company/family to other companies/families is the wrong approach.

Comparing our actual performance to our potential performance is the right approach. To do this, we must take the time to discover our potential and then set the bar at that level. We need to use *our* bar, not simply the bar that represents the "industry norm"…because clearing a bar is inconsequential if that bar is someone else's.

>>   PERSONS IN UNBALANCED ORGANIZATIONS DO NOT ACHIEVE THEIR POTENTIAL—AND THEREFORE NEITHER DOES THE ORGANIZATION.

There's a story about a man who wanted to help build a house. The builder asked him to cut 100 boards, each eight feet long. He measured the first and cut it. He used the cut board to measure the next board. He then used board #2 to measure for board #3, then board #3 for board #4. He continued that process until he had cut all 100 boards. What was the result? The final boards were nearly nine feet long because each time he measured using the previous board, his cut was slightly longer.

Greatness isn't born externally. Greatness doesn't arrive by being a little better than the one standing beside us, a little better than our competitors. Greatness is born internally; it lives inside you, your organization. Greatness arrives when we find and maximize our potential. Greatness doesn't come by measuring ourselves against the board that was cut by our competitors but rather by measuring our own board and letting that inspire us. Measuring yourself against someone else requires discipline and motivation, which is hard work. Measuring yourself against your potential is inspiring—and what brings contentment and enthusiasm to your life and to your organization. Start being great today!

Over-managed, Under-led

I used to attend a church that displayed the classic characteristics of an over-managed and under-led organization. The senior pastor was a great orator, a gifted teacher, and a strong manager, but he was not a good leader. He tried very hard to lead the church, but, in the first few years I attended, the church had a new authentic story each year—meaning there was no "sticking power," no impact realized by the previous stories. The only thing the congregation could be sure of was that there would be another, different destination coming next year, which resulted in a marginally effective church. Did people show up on Sundays? Yes. Did the community know the church existed? Certainly. However, did the church have a lasting impact for God's Kingdom? No, in my opinion. Why not? The answer is clear to me: The organization was unbalanced, with many managers and few leaders.

I am convinced that most organizations fall into the over-managed and under-led category...because, in effect, managing "feels" better than leading, for most of us. Figure 3.5 depicts the progression spelled out below. I believe we all go through this cycle that drives us to feel more comfortable managing than leading:

1. We learn to manage before we learn to lead;

2. We feel in control when we manage;

3. When we are in control, we believe fewer mistakes will occur;

4. Management is measurable, so we can demonstrate success;

5. Leadership is never easy, as it requires thinking, innovation, and change;

6. Thinking often feels unproductive, and others may not embrace change in the organization;

7. Leadership is difficult to measure;

8. Leadership success is hard to demonstrate, making leadership uncomfortable;

9. Thus, we move toward comfortable...so we manage (do!) something. (My wife is going to ask me what I accomplished this week, and I want to tell her something!)

We learn to manage before we learn to lead. From the time we are little, we are given things to manage: our room, a pet, simple chores, etc. We learn to make a daily list of tasks and to check them off as we complete them. Showing "accomplishment" by checking items off a list conditions us to believe that being able to show accomplishment (in this case, by completing task lists) is a good thing, a good management technique.

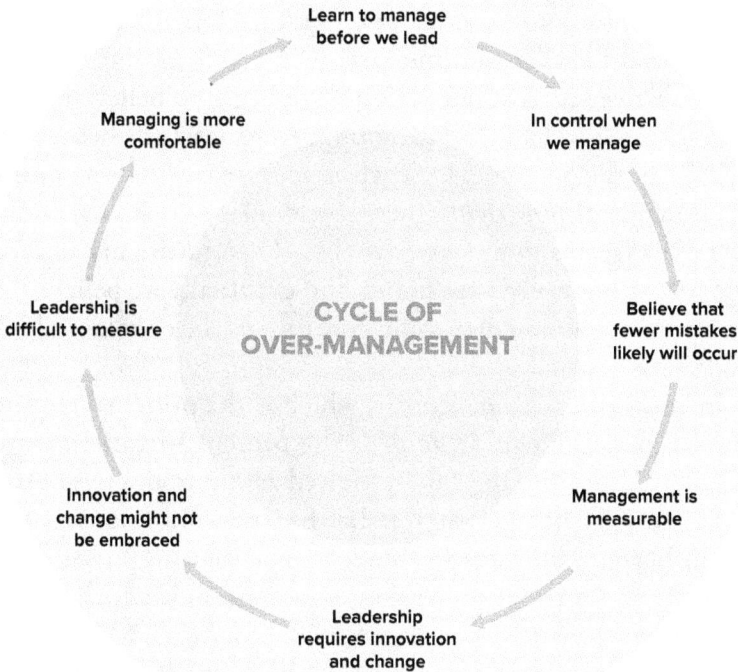

Learn to manage
before we lead

Managing is more
comfortable

In control when
we manage

Leadership is
difficult to measure

CYCLE OF
OVER-MANAGEMENT

Believe that
fewer mistakes
likely will occur

Innovation and
change might not
be embraced

Management is
measurable

Leadership
requires innovation
and change

Figure 3.5 – Cycle of Over-Management

(In 1988, the movie *Action Jackson* was released. I would be a little surprised if you saw it, but who am I to judge?! Action Jackson, played by Carl Weathers, was a super cop who saves the day multiple times like the heroes in all good action flicks do. Everyone wants a nickname like "Action Jackson." Again, we are conditioned/convinced that *action* is the key. We all want to be around people who get things done, and there are worse things to be known for...so overall, being considered the "action person" is not bad. Of course, taking action is important, but the effectiveness of action(s) is dependent on the reason why those actions are taken.)

In our careers, the management mentality progression continues because we are rewarded, or find success, as "list-checker-offers." We receive promotions based upon past performance, not upon future potential. We find mentors who reinforce our thinking that "effectiveness is about action." We begin to believe that we are best suited to handle critical opportunities/tasks because we can control the outcome. Delegating soon ceases to be an option because control *feels right*. The age-old adage "If it ain't broke, don't fix it" seems to fit. We have this "I can justify my actions" dialogue with ourselves for hours, and eventually we believe that managing—retaining maximum control—is the only logical way to proceed.

In contrast to *action/activity*, which is the principal requirement of management, *thinking* is the principal requirement of leadership. But thinking can be viewed as "unproductive." After all, starters do not get the credit; finishers do—so we often seek to become finishers (we endeavor to climb up, not climb down, as we are conditioned that we should finish at the top in organizations).

Furthermore, if we spend time thinking, and if people do not like our ideas, then the time we spent thinking seems pointless—and hence, what value are we providing to the organization? And even if people like our thinking, our leadership story, we may never actually witness our "complete picture," because change can take years.

Consequently, we can reach the point when we determine that leadership is indeed what we *should* be doing...but we become persuaded that leadership doesn't feel right and/or that we don't have time to lead. So, we return—full force—to managing. After all, managing seems easier than leadership, and management is certainly easier to measure than leadership (as evidenced by the statement "shareholders expect results, so results are what we'll give them"). Hence, the vicious cycle continues.

If you see yourself or your organization spinning on the management cycle, know that you are over-managing. I realize that the conventional term for "over-managing" is "micro-managing."

Micro-managing is a negative term, but if we consider its opposite, *macro-managing*, to be a positive term, we'd be missing the point altogether. So, I would encourage you to not think of "over-managing" as "micro-managing" (or as "macro-managing" for that matter); instead, allow *over-managing* to indicate that the correct behavior is being applied but in the wrong amount—whether too much, as in the case of micro-managing, or too little, as in the case of macro-managing.

Over-management generally results in an organization that is underperforming, employs people who don't feel empowered, exhibits little accountability, and delivers no measurable impact to its market. Applied to the family, over-management results in limited communication, friction between parents and children, and children seeking leadership in other places.

>> *OVER-MANAGING* INDICATES THE CORRECT BEHAVIOR IS BEING APPLIED BUT IN THE WRONG AMOUNT.

BREAK OUT, BREAK THROUGH

If you agree with any of what's been presented thus far, the next logical question is, "How can we stop the over-management cycle that is prevalent in many organizations?"

I believe the answer, in part, is found in the fact that people are wired *both* to lead and manage.

Let's start physically with our chemical constitution. We have many chemicals within our bodies, but four of these are endorphins, dopamine, oxytocin, and serotonin. What do these chemicals do?

My wife and I have run several marathons together. Her first marathon was in Indianapolis, Indiana. Somewhere around mile eighteen, I was looking for a bus to step in front of to take me out of my misery while my wife was running circles through the water stop telling me, "Suck it up!" Her endorphins were flowing more than mine. Endorphins block pain so we can complete a task. You've heard the term "runner's high." I've heard it too but have never experienced it. The runner's high stage of the race is when a runner pushes through the pain and finishes the race.

Dopamine is the chemical that makes us feel good when we check something off a list. My wife is a list checker-offer. She loves to make a list and complete it, sometimes to the extreme of completing something, adding it to her list, then checking it off! Dopamine and endorphins allow us to get things done; they are management chemicals.

The chemicals oxytocin and serotonin are generated when we are loved or have relational success, like when we have a great conversation or connect with someone. They are not instantaneous chemicals like endorphins and dopamine but are related to how relationally connected we become over time. They are leadership chemicals.

Let's take this a step further and look at how we were created and what we were given as part of that creation. Of course, some of you reading this will dismiss the premise that humans are "created" beings. If you are one who disagrees with the creation story, I challenge you to do your research in the first book of the Bible. In that book, Genesis, the first chapter discusses the concept of *dominion*—that humans are assigned dominion over the earth. Dominion in this context is taken from a Hebrew word that contains the ideas of leadership, management, mastery of skills, and governance.[2]

If the Genesis account is true, then in all of us resides leadership and management…not at the same potential but certainly at some capacity. Consequently, the first step toward breaking the cycle of over-management is **believing we can lead**—which means changing the way we think about leadership.

The second step is that we need to see others the same way as our (new) view of ourselves. That is, instead of seeing others as incapable of managing or leading effectively, we should explore how we can unlock the potential for leadership and management within them.

Finally, we must ask ourselves the questions I posed in the previous chapter: "Are we leading, and should we be?" and "Are we managing, and should we be?" Routinely asking these questions will slow us down and compel us to be thoughtful about our next action. Asking these questions routinely should also compel us to seek additional understanding of both leadership and management.

GET YOUR BALANCE

So, think about your life, your family, your organization for a few moments. Where do you see balance? Where do you see imbalance? Not sure? If you don't know what to look for, the chart on the following page (Table 3.1), while not all-inclusive, will provide you with some metrics for evaluation.

How can this table help you? Well, let's say, for instance, that you have very little trust in your family. Do your kids trust you, or are they just doing what you ask merely to avoid confrontation? If the latter is true, perhaps this is the case because you have an unbalanced organization—too much management by mom and dad and not enough leadership. The same may be true of your organization. Look, I am not trying to act as an antagonist here... but trust me in that leadership and management, applied at the right time and in the right amounts, can radically change your organization or family. How do I know this? I have seen it in my own life, both at work and home.

In summary, balanced organizations are: focused on purpose not power, have employees who are doing things that align with their skills, and effective in delegating responsibility, authority, and accountability—which results in high employee engagement and retention, because employees can see organizational progress and experience being a valuable part of that progress.

Unbalanced organizations, in contrast, are focused on titles and positional power, have people with high management acumen in positions requiring high leadership acumen, and ineffective in delegating responsibility, authority, and accountability (though they may desire to do so), which results in low employee retention and organizational progress—because employees are disengaged and confused.

Table 3.1 – Balanced and Unbalanced Organizations

Balanced	Over-Managed / Under-Led	Over-Led / Under-Managed
The organization understands the story, and people find their place in the story.	The story may be clear at the top but is opaque within the broader organization. People are writing their own story to fill the void.	A story is clear, but the organization lacks people to write the chapters. It's a story that exists primarily on paper with little reality.
A consistent management framework exists within the organization.	People view their value as problem solvers. Consistent processes are lacking, and crisis management prevails.	There is little emphasis on processes because the story is strong enough to "get things done."
Power is as a "hot rock." Hold it too long, and you will get burned.	Power is a result of one's position: you have the position, you have the power.	Power coexists with the best idea. If you have the best idea, you hold the power.
There is a balance between direction and action.	Action is abundant but an insufficient amount of direction.	There is an abundance of direction with an insufficient amount of action.
Purpose drives processes.	Process drives purpose.	Purpose reigns supreme such that processes seem unnecessary for success.
Trust is evident, and the story inspires the organization.	Trust is lacking. People focus on what's good for them.	Trust is evident, but actions are more discipline or motivated than inspired.
The character of the organization is displayed through its culture.	The character of the organization wavers as results dominate character.	The character of the organization is individual, not the collective.
The actions of the organization are driven by its inspiration.	The actions of the organization are driven by short-term results.	The actions of the organization start inspired but lack drive for completion.
Potential-based promotion is focused on success in the next position.	Time-based promotion is based on employee's network or length of service.	Limited promotion is due to lack of organizational depth.

FINAL THOUGHTS

I like to play with my grandkids at the park. Swinging and sliding are fun, but getting on the seesaw has always been my favorite. However, my young grandkids become a little frightened when they see a 200-plus pound "Pop-Pop" sitting on the seesaw across from their 35-pound frame. Why does this scare them? They don't understand that different distances can balance different weights.

I hope you now better understand balance, though…balance between leadership and management. Such balance is required for all organizations—and individuals—to maximize their potential.

If you are wondering about your organizational balance, perform a quick evaluation by using Table 3.1. Of course, evaluating your organization's condition requires an understanding of both leadership and management, which I trust you now have!

From here on in, this book will focus on leadership, not management. Numerous good management books can help you manage more effectively, and if becoming an awesome manager is what you are looking for, *Climbing Down* will disappoint you. However, if you want to understand how to examine your current leadership skills logically and how to take some tangible steps daily to improve those skills, I am confident that you will find value in the remainder of our journey together.

4

IT'S ALL IN YOUR HEAD

When I was a kid, I hated Friday nights. That might strike you as odd…a kid who hates Friday evenings. Okay, so *technically* I did not hate Friday night in and of itself; what I hated about Friday night is that it was the night before Saturday morning—when I had my dreaded piano lessons (which were doubly dreadful those weeks when I didn't practice). I would magically come down with an illness every Friday, to which my mother would often say, "Your sickness is all in your head!" Well, she was correct; I was never sick…other than sick of playing the piano. In hindsight, I wish I had put more effort into those lessons so that I could tickle the ivories today; instead, I spent part of my childhood being "sick."

Have you convinced yourself you are NOT a leader? Unfortunately, many people have convinced themselves of this, and that is why this chapter is here—to address how our thinking impacts our potential, including our leadership potential.

RENEWABLE RESOURCE

Our thinking drives our behavior. There are plenty of empirical studies to support that claim, and most of us would agree with that statement based on our experience alone. Thinking is at the center of everything we do. Wrong thinking often results in undesirable outcomes, and right thinking frequently produces positive results. Thus, how we think is critically important to how we live our lives and the impact we have on those around us.

To state that you can't change behavior by *trying* to change behavior would be disingenuous—because you can. However, that change is almost always short term. Let's look at some examples.

I spent seventeen years in the power industry. In that industry, safety is a critical issue, and toward improving a plant's safety culture, a common approach is to add more training, more tasks, additional oversight, and more assessments/inspections. Yes, taking that approach may enhance some aspects of a safety program, but that approach does not produce permanent improvements. Why? Simply "doing" safety-related functions without a change in safety thinking will not produce lasting change—because executing the many other operational tasks required to run a power plant will eventually shift focus off safety functions, which will cause the safety culture to return to its previous level.

Similarly, I have tried many different diet plans. I lost weight on every plan…that is until the weight came back quicker than it came off! The weight came back because I had no change in thinking regarding healthy living—I only had a desire to change my appearance.

Leadership is no different. As leaders, how we think will determine the success we have in leading others, regardless of the circumstances or settings in which we lead. Simply put, if I think I do not have any leadership skills, then I will not lead. Likewise, if I think I understand leadership but do not, I will try to lead but will hit brick walls around every corner.

The apostle Paul, who wrote much of the Bible's New Testament, addressed thinking in his letter to the Romans, wherein he said, "Do not conform to the pattern of this world but be transformed by the renewing of your mind" (Romans 12:2). To *renew* means "returning something to its original condition, making it new again." So, in using that word, Paul was encouraging the Roman people to *stop* thinking about religious rituals and to *start* thinking about connecting with their created purpose, as described in Genesis, the first book of the Bible.

>> SIMPLY PUT, IF I THINK I DO NOT HAVE ANY
LEADERSHIP SKILLS, THEN I WILL NOT LEAD.

WATCH AND LEARN

Most of what we think about leadership comes from experience, trying to lead and being led. Our thinking about leadership, however, might need to be renewed, to be cleansed from the wrong images of leadership we have in our minds. How did we develop wrong thinking regarding leadership? The same way all wrong thinking generally develops: by observation.

Our observations of leadership occur primarily via on-the-job training (OJT)—from our parents, teachers, coaches, youth leaders, etc. We are conditioned to believe that what we observe is "good" leadership and management. In some cases, the leadership we observe is good, and in other cases, bad. Consequently, our concept of what constitutes effective leadership is often contingent upon the organizations (families, businesses, sports teams) in which we first encountered leadership. That said, we can easily see how this dynamic can shortchange our understanding of what proper leadership should look and act like.

For instance, when parents repeatedly instruct children to do something using "because I said so," children perceive that leadership means "power"—so if they want to be a good leader, they need to achieve enough power to tell people what to do. On the other hand, a coach or teacher who encourages children to dream big and to connect with their gifts paints a proper picture of leadership...and sets children on a course to accomplish great things. This contrast between poor and proper pictures of leadership illustrates the problem with OJT through observation. Entering a situation, we don't know if what we will observe is a poor picture of leadership or a proper one.

Consequently, our OJT is somewhat left to chance.

Like purchasing a lottery ticket.

Perhaps in your OJT you will win the leadership lottery and be surrounded by great leaders. But I must ask: What are the odds of winning a lottery? The likelihood in OJT is that you will encounter less-than-adequate leaders. And the danger is that being new to leadership, you will not realize that the picture these inadequate leaders paint is a poor one, as you will have nothing against which you can compare their leadership.

For example, when I joined the United States Navy, I did not have an abundance of experience with leadership. Hence, I assumed the person commanding the submarine *had* to be a good leader. What I found puzzled me, though. The commander did not inspire, lacked a vision, and seldom gave me a reason to follow—other than because the "leader" held the title of captain. How could that be? How could the individual responsible for a $1 billion nuclear submarine, with 130 officers and crew capable of inflicting significant damage, be a below-average leader? Or worse, a non-leader?

The lesson here is that basing our understanding of leadership through experience or OJT is a real problem because we cannot tell if leadership is good or bad if we don't know what a good standard should look/feel/act like. When we lack a reference point, the more we see something, the more it can become the accepted practice, the new normal…and we are left unaware that our thinking on leadership is wrong because we have seldom witnessed the right way to lead. Fortunately for me, poor examples of leadership launched me on a quest for answers, a quest I've been on for more than thirty years. What I've discovered on that quest has shaped much of what I'm sharing with you in this book.

COMPUTE THIS!

As Dr. Caroline Leaf and others have written extensively, we have a conscious and non-conscious mind. The conscious mind works slower and only when we are awake, whereas the non-conscious mind works much faster and 24/7. When negative thoughts get written into our non-conscious mind, they tend to overrun thoughts in our conscious mind. For example, your action-oriented, purpose-pursuing thinking may have been stunted by a parent who said you couldn't do something, or a coach who said you would never amount to anything, or a "friend" who told you to forget your dream, or a spouse who reminded you that, since you had a family to raise, you had to park your passion until your kids left the house. Simply put, until you can change your mind—*renew* your mind, think differently, and allow renewed thinking to drive your beliefs—your dreams will remain wishes, and your frustration will remain a reality.

Our minds work like computers. Our conscious mind is our temporary, random access memory (RAM) that works when we are awake and then "resets" when we are asleep. Our non-conscious mind is our permanent, hard drive memory that is available twenty-four hours a day and retains what has been saved.

If (*when*!) our computer has a problem, a typical fix is to reboot the system; rebooting resets the RAM but has no impact on the hard drive. Along with rebooting, we employ other measures to facilitate the health of our computers.

- Right Environment – We put our computer in the "right" environment, where encountering a virus is unlikely. When online, we do this by verifying websites are legitimate and safe before accessing them.

- Quick Scans – Many computers do a quick scan to ensure the primary files and programs are free of defect and operating correctly.

- Full Scans – At prescribed intervals, many computers scan every file, folder, and program in the system to assess proper functionality.

- Quarantined Files – During scans (quick or full), any abnormal files that can't be fixed are quarantined—separated to prevent the infection of other data or programs.

- Operating System Updates – Periodically, the central operating system and other programs require an update to address problems that have been identified.

We can glean some useful information about our thinking by applying how our computers "think."

- Right Environment – If we want to change the way we think, we need to hang around with people who think differently than us—who think the way we *aspire* to think. Said another way, if you want to be a better leader, hang out with better leaders.

- Quick Scans – We can quickly scan our minds by pausing and asking ourselves a question or two. This momentary pause, a quick scan of our current thinking, helps us to make a thinking change if needed.

- Full Scans – Occasionally, we need to perform a deep dive of our thinking through attending a seminar, reading a book, and/or finding a mentor.

- Quarantined Files – When we pause to ask ourselves a question or to do a deep dive in our thinking, any wrong thinking needs to be quarantined, set aside until it can be removed. Basically, this means you stop thinking thoughts that you have identified as wrong.

- Operating System Updates – Finally, once wrong thinking is removed, we need to replace that thinking with new or renewed thinking. Removing old thinking in required, but the old thinking will likely return unless we replace it with new thinking.

OUTSIDE IN OR INSIDE OUT?

Humans are created with a spirit, a soul, and a body. Our spirit is what connects us to the Creator; our soul is the center of reasoning, housing our will, emotions, and cognition; and our body is the physical shell that delivers externally what is happening internally.

In *Start With Why*,[1] Simon Sinek discusses inside-out and outside-in thinking. Inside-out thinking centers on purpose and outside-in thinking centers on results. Extrapolating from this, we can either function inside-out (spirit to soul to body) or outside-in (body to soul to spirit).

Because the physical is the only visible aspect of our humanity, we tend to spend more time focused on our physical body and less time on our soul and spirit. Therefore, we are inclined to examine our behavior before we examine our thinking, and we often *only* look at behavior and neglect our thinking.

Here's the good news. We can change that! We can become inside-out focused and change the way we function by changing the way we think—by focusing on our purpose, on where we want to go, instead of wallowing in where we are now and worrying about what tomorrow might bring.

Below, the specific emphasis concerns how we think about leadership.

Two Sides of the Leadership Coin

Before we can change our leadership thinking, we first need to examine our current thoughts on leadership. You may identify with one or several of these prevailing ideas about leadership.

- Leadership is power. – A leader compels others to conform to his/her will, ideas, directions, etc.

- Leadership is about position. – With a certain position or title comes both real and perceived power to get things done. Thus, when I get into a "leadership position," I will lead.

- Leadership requires direct reports. – Leaders can't lead without people, so I can't lead until I have subordinates.

- Leadership requires special DNA. – I'm just not wired to lead; I'm just better at being told what to do and then getting things done.

- "Leadership is influence—nothing more, nothing less." – A popular leadership expert states this, so this claim must be true.

- "Leadership is the capacity to translate vision into reality." – Another popular leadership expert states this, so this claim must be true.

- Leadership requires charisma. – Leaders gain followers because they are the center of attention and willing to be out front.

Let me add some additional perspective to the above conceptualizations of leadership.

- Leadership is power. – Positional leaders see leadership as power. They believe they have earned that position and the power associated with their title.

- Leadership is about position. – There is no hierarchy to leadership. In other words, whoever is telling an authentic story and gaining trust is leading...whether the CEO or the newest employee in the organization.

- Leadership requires direct reports. – Again, there is no hierarchy to leadership; having followers does not have to mean that you have direct reports.

- Leadership requires special DNA. – All humans are created with the capacity to lead and to manage. The question is: How do people activate their leadership potential?

- Leadership is influence. – John Maxwell is a notable leadership expert who says that the true measure of leadership is influence, nothing more or nothing less. I think that statement can be misconstrued to make *influence* the focus of leadership. Thus, I'd alter this claim to by stating the *result* of leadership is influence; lead well, and you will be an influencer.

- Leadership is the capacity to translate vision into reality. – This statement is from Warren Bennis, another leadership expert. I like what he says but would add two words—"and management"—to his claim. I believe that leadership *and management* are the capacity to translate vision into reality, with vision pertaining to leadership and reality pertaining to management.

- Leadership requires charisma. – Charisma is a gift, and, yes, charisma can be very useful for leading. However, charisma is not the only gift pertinent to leadership.

Soldiers in battle frequently have to deal with "the fog of war," which is clouded judgment resultant from the chaos of battle. Related to this phenomenon, the chaos of life—work, family, social, etc.—can cloud our ability to improve our leadership. Normally, we don't, or can't, take time to assess what we think about leadership and if those thoughts are accurate...which is why I provided a point/counter point examination of leadership thinking. The takeaway from this exercise is that you have permission to think differently. You don't have to think like me, Maxwell, Bennis, or anyone else. But you *do* have to understand why you think the way you do. Your behavior will follow your thinking, so think the way you desire to behave and make no apologies for it.

Initiate a full scan on the hard drive of your mind. If you discover some incorrect thinking on leadership, you have to quarantine and remove those incorrect thoughts (don't continue to think them), so you can replace them with new, correct leadership thoughts—and enhance your capacity to lead.

FINAL THOUGHTS

Because thinking drives behavior, your potential is inseparable from how you think. Specifically, your thinking on leadership—comprised of what you've observed in other leaders and your experiences in leading and following—might be limiting your ability to lead.

For instance, if you *don't* think you have the ability to lead, you're right (even though your thinking is incorrect). But if you *do* think you have the ability to lead, you're also right. So, to fully realize your leadership potential, make sure your thinking is—and remains—renewed, or you might find yourself "sick" on a Friday night, wishing you had practiced the piano a little more!

5

LADDER CLIMBING:
Bring Up a Pack of Shingles

My dad was a college physics professor. This career gave him time in the summer to work on various projects around our house. One summer, he decided the garage needed new shingles. Now, most fathers want to pass along skills to their kids, and my dad was no different. He wanted my brother and me to be involved, to gain experience that we might use later in life.

Due to an early workout session for high school football, I missed the beginning of the roofing project but observed an interesting dynamic between father and son upon my return. My brother, Jon, had a pack of shingles on his shoulder and was attempting to ascend the ladder. His goal was to deliver the shingles to the roof, where our dad was waiting to start the installation process. However, Jon seemed stuck about halfway between the ground and roof, with one hand on the ladder and the other supporting the shingles. His legs were shaking; he was struggling mightily to take the next step.

What does this story have to do with this book? Well, this anecdote paints a vivid mental picture...and I always enjoy busting on my brother! But the main point is this: Leaders often think their leadership ladders are for climbing *up*, and in that upward climb leaders sometimes struggle to reach the next rung due to fear, fatigue, and/or frustration.

We are conditioned to believe we need to move higher in life. Hence we need to climb up something—even if that climbing requires us to step on a few people who are on the ladder with us. Sitting in the corner office one day is the goal, which predicates climbing up, with each new rung defining our success. The problem is that we almost never look *down* the ladder as we climb up; thus, when we finally arrive at the top, we realize that no one else is with us. Since we do not have anyone following us, the top tends to be a lonely place.

My brother finally did arrive at the top of the ladder with the shingles and found the return trip down the ladder much easier; because he left his burden on the roof and because gravity aided his descent to his destination (solid ground!). Picture your leadership journey as you climb down the ladder, lightening your load as you gain willing followers, empowering others along the way, scattering seed for your legacy, and reaching your destiny. Working smarter not harder and climbing down are the wise way to lead!

The remainder of this chapter will explain why a ladder is an accurate portrayal of how to view leadership and will explore movement along the ladder—the results of which will be further unpacked in subsequent chapters.

>> WORKING SMARTER NOT HARDER AND CLIMBING DOWN ARE THE WISE WAY TO LEAD!

LADDERS

Two primary components comprise a ladder: the rungs (the horizontal pieces) and the rails or stringers (the vertical pieces). Typically, all the rungs are the same width, and the two rails are the same length, providing stability for the ladder. Some ladders also have feet, two pieces at the bottom of the rails that balance load distribution, providing additional support. Ladders come in a variety of materials, colors, and weights. The thickness and material of the rails and rungs determine a ladder's duty—the weight a ladder can safely hold.

Now, I know I am describing a common piece of equipment with which you are familiar, but you may have just learned something previously unknown by looking at a ladder from a different viewpoint. Maybe you were unaware that the vertical pieces of a ladder are called rails, or maybe you had never realized ladders were classified by different weight restrictions. Note: We can often use a piece of equipment or a tool for a long time and still learn something new about it when we examine it from a fresh perspective. That's what we are going to do with the stages of leadership, too. We are going to examine the stages from a different perspective, with the purpose of providing a new understanding that should help you to lead more effectively.

There are various kinds of ladders, but the basic function of each is to help us reach something that would otherwise remain out of reach. From hanging Christmas lights to entering a submarine to carrying new shingles up to the roof, ladders are the vehicles that allow us to accomplish an objective that would otherwise be difficult or impossible to achieve. Don't miss this! The reason a ladder is an appropriate metaphor for leadership is that leadership, like a ladder, allows us to arrive at a destination that would otherwise be off our map, out of reach. Leadership elevates an organization to a place where that which was once high and lofty is now at eye level; leadership allows us to gain momentum, movement.

(If you have been unable to produce sustained superior results within and through your organization, you need to look at your leadership. We often believe we can manage our way out of mediocre results or poor performance, but doing this never works. Whether within your organization, within your family, or within your own heart and mind, balancing leadership and management is the only way by which you will reach and sustain a superior level of performance, develop admirable family dynamics, or permanently affect the lives of those you encounter along life's journey.)

Ladders are constructed using various materials and painted using various colors. These different colors and materials, however, do not change the overall purpose of the ladder—to allow one to climb! Relatedly, those on the leadership ladder are constructed from different "materials" (backgrounds, experiences, education levels), and have been painted various colors by the Creator; these differences are beautiful in and of themselves and reveal a beautiful thing about the leadership ladder—it accommodates *anyone* who wants to develop his/her God-given ability to lead.

>> LEADERSHIP ELEVATES AN ORGANIZATION TO A PLACE WHERE THAT WHICH WAS ONCE HIGH AND LOFTY IS NOW AT EYE LEVEL.

ONWARD AND DOWNWARD

The rungs of the leadership ladder (Figure 1.1, p. 6) represent the five stages of leadership. As with most other ladders, you traverse the rungs on the leadership ladder sequentially, and you can move in both directions—but if you remain on any rung too long, people may start to look to others for leadership.

That said, two factors impact your location on the leadership ladder. First, you occupy different rungs with different people within your organization. For instance, you may accept a new role within the organization and find yourself necessarily moving from the *people development* rung (where you were with your previous team) to the *position* rung, as you start over with a new team. Second, your decisions and ability to communicate impact which rung you occupy. For example, you may be at the *production* rung of the leadership ladder but act in a way that is disconnected from the story and consequently move back up to the *permission* rung.

The rails of the leadership ladder represent the mechanisms, actions necessary to climb down from one rung to the next. Doing these actions well will allow you to move down the leadership ladder, and not doing them well—or not doing them at all—will either strand you on a rung or move you back up one or more rungs toward the top of the ladder.

Note that in the leadership ladder diagram, one of the rails is labeled *Leader* and the other is labeled *Follower*, indicating that leaders don't—can't—move down the ladder without followers. A leader moving separately from his/her followers is like a ladder with rails of different lengths. Such a ladder is disproportionate, not sturdy, unable to safely support the required weight. A leader who moves without followers is out of step, and, according to John Maxwell, simply someone out for a walk.

Below is a summary of the corresponding leader-follower actions that facilitate movement down the ladder.

To move to the *permission* rung of the ladder, the leader must engage in *authentic storytelling*, and the follower must begin to *trust*. To move to the *production* rung, the leader must take *inspired action*, and the follower must accept *empowerment*. To move to the *people development* rung, the leader must establish *proven character*, and the follower must initiate *replication*. And to move to the *personhood* rung, the leader must share their *created purpose*, and the follower must begin to tell an *authentic story*.

Just like the weight restrictions for actual ladders are based on the thickness and type(s) of material used for rails and rungs, the stronger the material and thicker the rails and rungs on your leadership ladder, the more load your leadership can carry. For example, when you first start moving along the leadership ladder, your rails and rungs will be thin; you'll gain just enough trust to move from *position* to *permission*, and you'll empower just enough people to help you gain momentum on the *production* rung. But as you continue to tell authentic stories and take actions inspired by those stories, trust will continue to strengthen, permitting the trust rail to carry more weight; and as more followers accept the empowerment you've offered, the empowerment rail will grow thicker, allowing your ladder to support an increasingly robust influence load.

As a result of climbing down the leadership ladder, you will achieve some milestones. These are *followers*, *history*, *legacy*, and *destiny*. In later chapters, I'll explain these milestones further. But for now, what I want to stress is that these milestones are the reasons one should strive to improve his/her leadership. After all, climbing down the leadership ladder just so that you can claim that you "improved" your leadership is inconsequential—because movement, in and of itself, is not important. What is important is the *result* of that movement.

FEET OF STRENGTH

Some ladders are too big for one person alone and thus require assistance to maneuver them into proper position (for maximum utility). Your leadership ladder should *always* be too big for one person alone…because your story should be bigger than just you! Leaders need followers in more ways than one. Yes, if you don't have any followers, you're not a leader—that's rather basic. But what I'm driving at here is that a leader needs *help* from an empowered team to position his/her ladder to reach the destination described in the authentic story.

And leaders not only achieve nothing without others' help but also achieve nothing without helping others. Part of the help you provide as a leader is developing followers so that they can (a) begin replicating what they have seen in your leadership and (b) begin constructing their own leadership ladders. As followers start to climb, they will need someone—you—to foot their ladder. This cycle…replication, footing, climbing down…starts with one leader who is willing to think differently, who understands that moving up the organizational chart means moving down the leadership ladder. Eventually, a follower replicates that one leader's thinking. Soon, three, then four, then six followers begin climbing down, and the replication cycle picks up momentum. And enough momentum produces a movement.

Footing a ladder means bracing the bottom of the ladder, thus securing the ladder for another to climb on it. You can foot a ladder either by standing inside the ladder (in between the ladder and the building/wall) or by standing outside the ladder. Either way, there are several things about footing an actual ladder that directly pertain to the leadership ladder.

- You are allowing others to climb.

- There is risk being at the bottom of the ladder.

- Securing the ladder takes strength.

- You can better foot a ladder if you have previously climbed a ladder.

- Whatever happens, you never let go of the ladder while someone is climbing.

The true impact of leadership resides at the intersection of allowing someone to help foot our ladder while helping others foot theirs.

Of course, I'm sure many of you have worked for someone who has allowed absolutely no one else to lay a hand on his/her leadership ladder. These folks are very poor leaders, people who enjoy their positional status, who make sure everyone knows they are "the boss." Perhaps *you* are that type of leader…and perhaps you are now wondering if there is a better way. Or perhaps you are asking, "Why does any of this matter?" To reiterate: Leadership's real impact and lasting potency are experienced when we have climbed down our ladder and begin holding others' ladders so they can climb down too. You can't foot a ladder from the top!

FINAL THOUGHTS

We are conditioned to think that climbing up the corporate ladder is always good and that climbing down is bad or wrong. Climbing down makes sense for leaders, however, as doing this helps them lighten their load (a) by empowering followers and (b) by turning followers into leaders through people development. In fact, I'm convinced that climbing down the leadership ladder will take you to heights you've never dreamed or imagined.

The leadership ladder allows us to evaluate our current leadership stage (rung) and defines actions (rails) for both leaders and followers to facilitate movement toward a lower rung. Why does moving down ladder require actions from both leader and follower?

Because leaders and followers need one another.

Unlike the NFL draft, when a team picks its players, leaders don't get to pick their followers. Rather, followers pick their leaders. This happens after the leader takes action, and the follower "chooses" (to follow) the leader through a corresponding action/reaction—allowing downward movement along the ladder to occur. Authentic storytelling is the starting place for the leader to gain trust from a follower. This action (storytelling) and reaction (trust) between leader and follower is the first of many mutual exchanges and interactions as the leader climbs down the ladder.

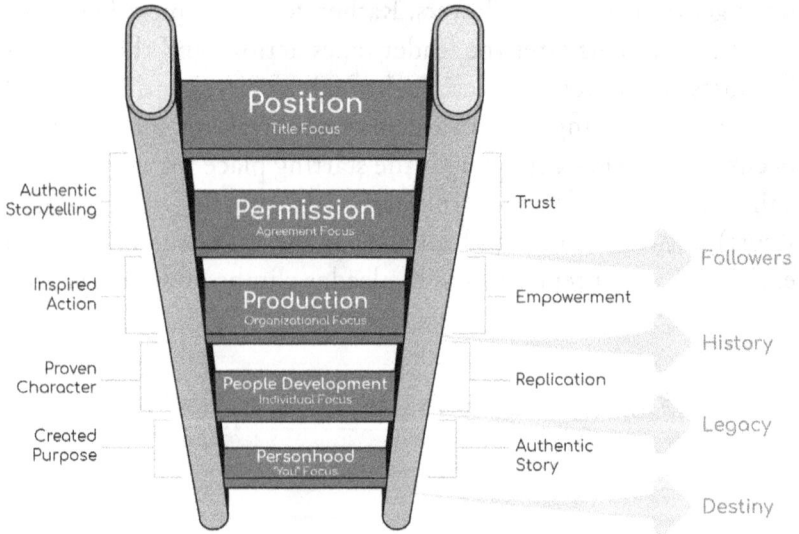

Leader | Follower

Position
Title Focus

Authentic Storytelling — Permission / Agreement Focus — Trust

Inspired Action — Production / Organizational Focus — Empowerment → Followers

Proven Character — People Development / Individual Focus — Replication → History

Created Purpose — Personhood / "You" Focus — Authentic Story → Legacy

→ Destiny

6

POSITION RUNG:
Because I Said So!

T.J. had just finished a hockey workout and flopped down on the couch to watch television in the living room. About fifteen minutes later, I walked in after a long day at the power plant and started small talk.

"How was your day, Teeg?"

"Good. Had a hard practice. Coach wasn't in a very good mood. What about you?"

"Typical day with the typical nonsense. Work would be a lot easier if everyone would just do their job. Anyway, are you still going to mow the yard?"

"Maybe tomorrow."

"It has to be done today, T.J. Mom has some people coming over tomorrow, and they will be outside."

I went into the bedroom to change clothes and to talk with Sharice. After about an hour, I realized the mower wasn't running and went to find T.J., who had progressed to playing on Nintendo. Honestly, I wasn't looking for an argument—but I wanted the grass cut, and I wasn't planning on doing it.

"T.J., go out and mow the yard, please."

"I don't feel like it, Dad. We had a hard practice."

"Get outside and mow, T.J.!"

"Why?" he challenged.

"Because I said so!"

There. That was it: *Because I said so!*—the phrase that I, when younger, had vowed never say to my kids.

Every parent has used that phrase at least once, and my wife and I raised three children while using that phrase more than we should have. When you say *Because I said so!*, you are telling your kids, "Follow me because you have no other choice. You didn't get to choose me to be your parent, so get over that and do what I tell you."

Sure, kids need some stern words at times—and so do the folks with whom we work. But we should recognize when we resort to language like *Because I said so!*, we are at the first stage of leadership—the top of the leadership ladder, the *position* rung.

This rung is the place where you must start as a leader and may be a place where you occasionally return on your leadership journey; however, the *position* rung is not a place where you should want to remain.

POSITIONAL RUNG LEADERSHIP

Positional leadership is exactly what it sounds like—you hold the title of "leader" only because of your position on the organizational chart. The same can be applied in your family: You are a positional leader because of your title as *father* or *mother*.

Having a title doesn't mean you are leading, though. Often, titles are not earned; often they're simply assigned labels that come with the role we're hired into or receive when a precious new life comes into the world carrying our DNA.

Positional leadership is not hard to understand, but spending a little time examining it is nonetheless worthwhile. Why? Because the better we understand positional leadership, the quicker we will want to leave it behind.

POWER PLAY

We are born with the capacity to exercise positional leadership (even though we may not understand what we are doing). You see positional leadership in kids from an early age. Take, for instance, a group of toddlers; before long, one of them attempts to impose his/her will on the others...regarding Cheerios, a toy, a particular seat on the floor, etc.

Imposing our will on others—dominating a conversation or exercising power—normally makes us feel good. Why do we have the innate desire to have power over someone else? We were created to be in power. Consequently, there is something that feels right about being a positional leader.

The idea of exercising power over another human being originated in the first three chapters of Genesis, the first book of the Bible. The first chapter of Genesis describes the creation of the earth and all its inhabitants, including humans. Additionally, this chapter provides humanity its chief assignment of having *dominion*—leadership and management—over all of creation except for other humans. Interestingly, if that idea conveyed in the first chapter of Genesis is correct (and I submit that it is), then although humans are to dominate birds, beasts, fish, plants, etc., we are *not* to dominate other humans. So why do we enjoy exercising power over each other today?

If you were to keep reading in Genesis, you would learn that in chapter three, a separation occurred between God and humanity. This separation is often referred to as the "fall of mankind." In a nutshell, the first humans decided to take action that was not authorized by God, and thus separation, fallout, occurred. You can understand this because we have all experienced a breach in our relationships; we disagree with another person, and then for a while being around one another feels awkward because we are misaligned in our ideas or opinions.

After that separation between God and humanity, the idea of leadership and management over the earth became distorted, and humans started trying to dominate each other. That phenomenon continues today and is the reason why positional leadership is so common. We are wired to have dominion (leadership and management), but we apply dominion incorrectly in trying to exercise power over each other.

Re-Positioned

Here is the challenge with positional leadership: You always start as a positional leader, and you are hardwired for dominion. The combination of positional leadership and dominion can be challenging in the quest to improve your leadership because you start at a place that feels good and you might not see the value in moving beyond your status as a positional leader.

Let's look at two examples.

You might be the best teacher in a school district in Michigan, but then you move to Florida. As a great teacher, you probably weren't simply a positional leader at your previous school because you understood something about leadership and moved down the ladder. However, few, if any, of your new colleagues in Florida know you were a great teacher in Michigan, and even if they were to learn this, they might not care. As an unknown quantity, you are merely a positional leader to them. So, you must start the process over—you must start climbing down again.

You might be running the production department of a small electronics manufacturer, leading empowered and engaged employees who are delivering outstanding performance. Because of your department's success, you are selected to revive the struggling sales and business development department. You become a positional leader again (within that new department), even though you are still in the same company. Leadership requires interaction at a level that impacts people, so even moving to another department can push you back to the top of the leadership ladder.

Some of you may think this doesn't sound very exciting—repeating the process over and over every time you move into a new organization or into a new role within the same organization. Why even work at becoming a better leader, then?

Well, your heart for climbing down is all about how you view change.

Change comes from the idea of exchanging or bartering. When you look at change as *exchange*—to take our ideas and trade or barter them with the ideas of new people—then the idea of going back to the top of the ladder isn't such a bad thing. In fact, starting over is a good thing because doing so allows you to... start over, to encounter fresh ideas that can ultimately continue to shape your authentic storytelling skills (we'll address this in the next chapter), making you an even better leader in the long run.

POSITIONAL RUNG OUTCOMES

Positional leaders have forced, fake followers. That is, people only follow positional leaders because—apart from finding another job or another family—following the positional leader is the only option.

Forced followers have some general characteristics: They tend to do only what is required of them, tell the leader only what he/she wants to hear, and look elsewhere for a leader to follow, even if that requires them to change jobs. We witness this dynamic play out very clearly within our families. When we resort to positional leadership as parents, our kids resist us in completing regular tasks—cleaning their rooms, making their beds, and doing their homework are a fight every night. Okay, maybe I am exaggerating about *every* night, but certainly, most of us have been on the giving or receiving end of positional leadership within a family.

Organizations tend to be only as good as their leaders. A positional leader is only a first-level leader, so his/her organization is only a first-level organization. Hence, there isn't an atmosphere of *going somewhere together*; instead, there's a *my way or the highway* environment. Trust is limited, and followers don't believe the story that is being told by the leader. Without trust, there is no synergy, and without synergy, the sum of the parts is not greater than the individual parts.

>> POSITIONAL LEADERS HAVE FORCED, FAKE FOLLOWERS.

Being "stuck" on the *positional* rung of the leadership ladder may not seem fair to you…because you may think that you are a good leader and agree that positional leadership is bad—yet you don't have people *willing* to follow you. Should that be the case, please let me help you with something: If you have no willing followers, stop thinking you're a good leader!

FINAL THOUGHTS

Operating on the *positional* rung is a requirement, a universal starting point for all leaders. However, those leaders who are consumed with—and by—power never leave the *positional* rung… and neither will you if you view a "leader" as the person who controls the most power. No one wants to be forced to follow, and true leadership—the kind that results in willing followers—is not about power but rather empowerment.

Followers *want* to connect with something bigger than themselves. Now, that doesn't mean a leader can never be direct, use a commanding style, or occasionally say, "Just do what I tell you." But that does mean that leaders who take the risk of releasing/sharing the power inherent to their position will facilitate different (more positive!) thoughts and actions within their sphere of followers.

7

FROM POSITION TO PERMISSION:
Story Time

If you want to move down the leadership ladder and be something other than a positional leader, *authentic storytelling* will facilitate that. You will gain willing followers—because people want to be part of something bigger than themselves.

What evidence do I have to back up that claim? Any crisis.

When a crisis occurs, people do things that they wouldn't do at any other day or time. Why? Mainly because crises demand that people join forces toward becoming part of something bigger, toward helping one another find a solution, toward accomplishing something not achievable on an individual level. For example, after September 11, 2001, there was a significant increase in military recruits because people wanted to be part of preserving the freedoms that we enjoy in the United States.

When I was in the navy, the phrase "it's time to go to sea" was used when the crew was starting to fragment and to not work well together. This phrase implied that a submarine tied to a pier isn't connected to its purpose and, hence, neither is its crew connected. Once we left for sea, though, the crew became focused, and the team came together again, as we all realized (again) our significance to the story and our purpose.

So what's your story? When you close your eyes and allow yourself to drift away, where do you go? You have a purpose—a destiny, or destination, for which you were created. You have seen it before. Capture it next time. Burn it into your memory. That is the story you want to tell. It will be inspiring, and it will connect with others.

Now, you may be wondering, "Can I truly understand why I was created, my purpose for existing?" Let me ask you this: Is there something you can do that comes naturally...that comes easier for you than for most? Is that activity, gift, or talent something you enjoy doing? The first step to understanding your purpose is identifying those things that you enjoy and that are easier for you than for others.

If you were going to create or invent something for a specific reason, you would probably build into that device everything it needed to perform that specific function. Humans are designed in the same way—the reason some things are easier for you than for others is that you were built for a different purpose and adequately equipped to fulfill that purpose. Simple as that. And simple as this: Birds are equipped to fly, fish are equipped to swim, and humans are equipped to achieve the destiny for which we are hardwired.

If the above paragraph is accurate, then why do people shy away from their story, from believing that they possess something the world needs? Fear, sacrifice, present capabilities, resources, time, etc. We can easily make a multiple-page list of why we are unwilling and/or afraid to dream big and to connect with our story. Conversely, and sadly, our reasons why we *should* connect with our story would probably fit on a sticky note.

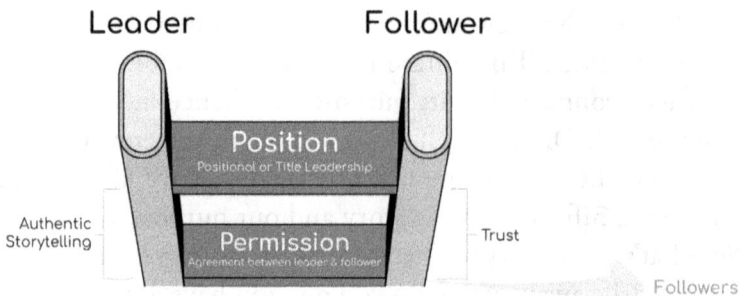

Leader   Follower

Position
Positional or Title Leadership

Authentic
Storytelling

Permission
Agreement between leader & follower

Trust

Followers

DESCENDING TO THE PERMISSION RUNG: LEADER'S ROLE

So...why take the risk of dreaming big and telling your story? Because improving your leadership begins with *authentic storytelling*. Why storytelling—and not *vision* or *excellence* or something along those lines? Instead of me providing the answer, I encourage you to try the following experiment.

Assemble a group of people from your organization (or gather your family in the living room) and tell them you want to talk about mission and vision. Scan the room and notice the number of people who have that "I'm acting like I'm listening while thinking about anything *other* than mission and vision" look. In my experience, numerous people in organizations and families fit this description.

Next, gather the same people at a different time and inform them that you want to tell them a story. Scan the room again and estimate the number of people who seem pleased or interested.

Here's why those two approaches yield different results: Many people consider *mission* and *vision* as things of interest to corporate executives rather than to typical employees. Conversely, almost everyone has a positive appreciation for a story. Without changing your entire leadership vocabulary, a simple moving from "mission and vision" to "story" might change the way your organization or family understands where it is going.

I'm a physics guy, so equations feel good to me. And in this case, an equation might feel good (and simple) to you, too:

$$Story = Mission + Vision$$

Again, if you prefer *mission* and *vision* that's fine, I'm simply suggesting *story* as an alternative. Why? Not everyone understands how to define—let alone, how to create—a vision and a mission, but everyone has read or heard a story. Not everyone understands how mission and vision affect their job, but everyone can identify with a character in a story.

Consequently, I believe that the first step to becoming a better leader seems more achievable if we frame that step in terms of storytelling. Think of it this way: To become a better leader, you do not have to morph into a "visionary" (that should be a relief). Rather, you simply need to develop an authentic story; and by telling this story, you will cast a vision and define a mission in a way that connects to listeners.

Of course, the content of your story needs to be compelling—the content needs to take people someplace, to a place that is better than where they currently are. But if you are not authentic, your story will simply seem a fairy tale. And if you don't communicate (tell) your story in the right way, it may simply seem like a drab instruction manual.

Let's further examine *authenticity* and *telling*, taking them in alphabetical order.

YOU BEING YOU

What makes a story authentic? What makes anything authentic? Authenticity is the idea of "original," not a copy.

People are willing to pay enormous amounts of money for an authentic Van Gogh painting or an original Babe Ruth rookie card. Others put forth incredible effort to find rare, authentic fossils.

Why does the authenticity of something matter? Because the concept of authenticity directly pertains to how we are created. You are unique; there is no one exactly like you. Even with billions of people alive today, you are not like any other human. Certainly, people possess similarities in appearance, skills, attitudes, etc., yet the "complete package" that is you is one of a kind. You are an original—authentically *you*.

So, who are you? (By asking this question, I hope to encourage your search for "you" to be an intentional one!)

Via technology, we can know, in part, our ancestry, who we are on a physical level. These days, many people seem quite enamored with understanding their lineage. Perhaps one driver behind this infatuation is that we believe knowing where we came from answers the question of where we should be going.

Certainly, your ancestry is important, but understanding your ancestry does not make you authentic. Here's why: Knowing your ancestry can provide insight as to why you look like you do (physical attributes) but knowing your ancestry does not reveal insight into how others "see" you (personal authenticity). Remember, authenticity originates inside of you and is made visible by your actions, behaviors, words, etc.—not by your appearance.

That is, ancestry is about you being associated with others, but authenticity is about you being you.

Authenticity is a precursor to believability, and believability is a precursor to trust. Trust is what leaders should be after; gaining a follower's trust is the reason to tell an authentic story. You won't be trusted if you are not believable, and you first have to believe your own story—because if *you* don't, others won't. This is similar to stating that you need to lead yourself before you can lead others.

WILLIAM TELL(ING) OVERTURE

What does originality, authenticity look like in our daily interactions? Telling the story in *your* words, in *your* way, through *your* perspective. That means you need to understand—not memorize—the story. Too many people think that having the right words, getting the story exactly correct, is the most important thing. The most important thing is understanding the intent of the story, so your originality, your authenticity, your believability is evident to those listening.

As we continue in our discussion of the telling of your story, I encourage you to fire up the jukebox in your mind.

The William Tell Overture is a composition you might be familiar with if you are a fan of classical music, or if you watched the 1950s western series, *The Lone Ranger*. Of course, the overture is the same music but played differently at the symphony than on the TV program.

Just as *The William Tell Overture* is used differently in different projects, you must be able to tell your story differently to connect with different people—because people understand and retain information differently. And just as the overture is the same music regardless of the setting, your message should remain the same regardless of your audience. The challenge is to maintain a consistent message while delivering it in a customized manner.

That is part of what makes *telling* so difficult.

>> AUTHENTICITY IS A PRECURSOR TO BELIEVABILITY, AND
BELIEVABILITY IS A PRECURSOR TO TRUST.

A critical component of communicating effectively is knowing your audience. Knowing your audience simply means that you understand how people best accept the communication, how they process information, and how they engage with what they hear/see/read.

We are all wired with default settings. Those default settings are called personality. Personality is simply what makes us the same but different, what makes us common but unique. For example: Sharice would often say on a Sunday afternoon, "You are in work mode again," recognizing that my default personality settings at home are different than at work. Is that difference okay? Certainly, because we all have the same suite of personality traits—but we aren't all wired with the same default settings! Therefore, those personality traits don't naturally manifest themselves the same.

Sometimes, a situation warrants us changing those default settings to shape an environment where the likelihood of the best outcome is increased. Understanding how others might respond is one of your responsibilities as a leader.

Which means—wait for it—you are required to get to know people! You need to watch how they respond in different situations and to listen to how they communicate. For instance...

I once worked for an owner who spoke in bullet points. We initially tried to communicate to him using a relational approach by asking questions like, "How was your weekend?" or, "What are your plans for a vacation this year?" Our approach drove the owner crazy—to the point that whatever we said after, "How was your weekend?" was completely ignored. We eventually realized that an effective way to interact with him was speaking in bullet points, just like he did. Did we change our message? No. But did we change our delivery mechanism? We certainly tried.

SHARE AND TELL

A shared experience is exactly as it sounds: Two or more people have some aspect of living life in common. (For instance, if you were in the navy, then you and I share that experience.) Finding common ground through shared experiences helps leaders in their telling of the story. Remember that in the *Climbing Down* leadership model "story" equates to mission/vision; therefore, our experiences are not part of our story, but these experiences certainly are a part of the *telling* of our story.

Here's how.

Our shared experiences help us connect with others, and that interpersonal connection increases the probability that the telling of the story will be more effective. I think of shared experiences as a "landing area" for our story, and the bigger the landing area we can create, the higher the probability that our story will be trusted.

In the small town where I grew up, carnivals came during the summer. One of the popular carnival games involved landing a ping-pong ball on a saucer. This, of course, was no easy task, because ping-pong balls are light and saucers are small. However, if one could replace the saucer with a serving platter, the game would become much easier. That is what shared experiences do in facilitating the telling of our story; shared experiences allow the saucer to grow to the size of a platter, resulting in a bigger, easier landing area for our story.

One point of clarification: Shared experiences have to be actual, real experiences. Making up an experience in an attempt to connect is a bad idea, a *really* bad idea. The goal is to gain trust, and deceiving someone is pretty much the opposite of being authentic, a precursor of trust. Sure, you can get away with fabricating a shared experience. But doing this puts you on borrowed time; you will eventually be exposed, and then gaining trust with the person(s) you initially deceived will be even more challenging than normal.

MAKING LASAGNA

My mother routinely made lasagna for college students: Noodles, ricotta cheese, sauce, and repeat. Layer after layer of sheer goodness!!

Authentic storytelling works the same way. For our organization to be effective from top to bottom, our stories must be layered, one on top of the other.

Let me illustrate this by using an example with which many are familiar: the speech Martin Luther King, Jr. delivered on August 28, 1963. This amazing speech was actually a sub-story, a story that fit under another story. King's speech fit under the story of the United States as recorded in the nation's founding documents—thus magnifying the power of King's message.

Many people have heard the "I have a dream…" portions of King's speech, but not as many can recall how his speech begins:

"In a sense we've come to our nation's capital to cash a check. When the architects of our Republic wrote the magnificent words of the Constitution and the Declaration of Independence, they were signing a promissory note to which every American was to fall heir. This note was a promise that all men—yes, black men as well as white men—would be guaranteed the unalienable rights of life, liberty, and the pursuit of happiness. It is obvious today that America has defaulted on this promissory note insofar as her citizens of color are concerned. Instead of honoring this sacred obligation, America has given the Negro people a bad check, a check which has come back marked "insufficient funds."

"But we refuse to believe that the bank of justice is bankrupt. We refuse to believe that there are insufficient funds in the great vaults of opportunity of this nation."[1]

Martin Luther King, Jr. was an extraordinary individual and a gifted orator, and I believe this particular speech had increased impact because it was a sub-story to one of the greatest stories ever told—the declaration by the founders of America that all persons were created equal and thus due specific and wonderful rights.

King's speech also teaches us that powerful stories are ones that are aimed at souls (emotions), not at roles (job functions). That is, a powerful story has a personal focus, not simply a personnel focus.

Leaders who tell powerful stories inspire followers to tell powerful stories. An important part of a leader's purpose, then, is assisting followers in (a) finding their personal story and (b) layering that personal story into the organization's story. Again, the story is mission plus vision, so each person's story is his/her personal mission and vision.

Helping people find and connect their personal story to the organization's story makes people feel valued. And doing this also *creates* value for the organization, because when people deliver what they are uniquely designed to do, their performance will improve, and the organization will benefit.

DESCENDING TO THE PERMISSION RUNG: FOLLOWER'S ROLE

For a leader to descend to the *permission* rung of the leadership ladder, followers have to trust the leader. Trusting the leader is different than believing the leader—as illustrated by Charles Blondin, a tightrope acrobat who lived in the late 1800s.

During Blondin's act, he would bring a wheelbarrow onto the tightrope and ask the crowd if they believed he could push this across to the other side. The crowd would go crazy with screams of, "Yes! You can do it!" Then came the follow-up question: Charles asked, "Who wants to get in?" You could hear a pin drop in the silence that followed—which illuminates the difference between belief and trust.

Belief is a thought; trust is an action. Specifically, trust is an initial belief that results in an action. In other words, belief moves the mind, but trust moves the body. The desired result of a leader's authentic story is that people begin moving through belief and into trust.

The word *trust* originates from the idea of a safe place, a place of refuge. A leader who tells an authentic story, then, invites followers to take refuge in the safety of the story...by describing a place that is better than the followers' current reality.

As noted, trust requires action, and the action required of followers is participation. That is, followers demonstrate that they trust the leader's authentic story by becoming active participants in, not merely interested observers of, the story.

>>   BELIEF IS A THOUGHT; TRUST IS AN ACTION.

FOLLOWING ISN'T FREE

That said, I have some bad news: Leaders will not gain followers from every audience with which they share an authentic story.

Because there is a cost to following a leader, and not all followers are willing to pay this cost.

Think of the leader-follower relationship in terms of a bank account. If a follower wants to be associated with a leader, he/she must make an initial deposit into the leader's "trust bank"—demonstrating the follower's confidence that (a) the leader's story is the right one and (b) the leader is authentic—and allow the leader to grow that deposit over time.

Here's a real-life example. When a candidate for office goes out on the stump, he/she attempts to tell an authentic story in hopes of receiving an initial deposit in his/her trust bank. As voters (followers), we may make this initial deposit, but we will have a hard time making future deposits (continuing to trust) if the candidate's message seems to change each time he/she addresses different groups—because even though the candidate's story sounded good at first, we soon struggle with the consistency of the candidate's story. We can't discern if the candidate is authentic or a chameleon that changes color based on the background behind the podium; so we withhold our trust, and the candidate doesn't have our permission (vote) to lead.

Earning a follower's trust is the only way to move to the *permission* rung of the leadership ladder—because followers must have a confident expectation that a leader's story is authentic and that the leader can create a better future. Remember: You don't go looking for followers; followers will find authentic storytellers and grant such leaders permission to lead. That is, people will willingly follow your leadership as they connect with your story and verify its authenticity.

The power of the right story told with authenticity exists in any organization, even in marriage. Guys, when courting your sweetheart, you tell her an authentic story for her to trust you—and make an emotional deposit in your relationship account. If she does trust you, and if you remain authentic, her deposit will continue to grow to the point where she might accept your marriage proposal—because she has bought into (a) the "story" that her life is better with you than without you and (b) your authenticity, that you are the "right" messenger. That is why dating is important. A lady needs time to validate the authenticity of a guy's story before she trusts him and gives him permission to marry her. This permission is the power of the follower.

FINAL THOUGHTS

The goal of leadership is not to gain followers—although the *result* of good leadership is indeed followers gained. Rather, the goal of leadership is to articulate your organization's story in such a way that others can see themselves as part of it. In such a way that they can see their skills and talents being put to good use. In such a way that they can see themselves as contributors to positive outcomes. When this happens, your organization is on the verge of transformation.

Authentic storytelling creates an opportunity for a follower to trust both the message and the messenger. Followers who put their trust in leaders find safety in the leader's story and thus become willing followers; willing followers allow leaders to move from the *position* to the *permission* rung of the leadership ladder. This is not to indicate, however, that forced followers (of positional leaders) aren't motivated or don't want to do a good job; rather, I'm saying that moving down cohesively—leaders and followers together—is very difficult in the absence of a story that describes a future destination.

Remember, authenticity is who you are, the story is your message, and telling is your delivery method. You can gain a few followers with a great story and little authenticity and/or with great authenticity and a marginal story. However, if you want to be a leader who climbs down—who creates a movement—you must be an authentic person who tells a great story.

8

PERMISSION RUNG:
"Permit-sion"

Every summer, my dad embarked on a building project. (As a college professor, he had many summers off from teaching.) One year, he decided to build a new garage after converting the original garage into a family room. Before starting the construction, he had to obtain a city permit, which was an agreement between the city and my father detailing the project to ensure that building codes would be followed. If he stayed within the boundaries of the permit, the city would allow the construction; building outside the permit parameters would incur penalties.

My dad hired a contractor to help pour the foundation for the new garage. Dad did all the work to set the forms and then patiently waited for the contractor to bring the concrete. His patience waned drastically, though, as the days turned into one week and then two. Finally, the day arrived for the foundation to be poured. I had the "privilege" of getting up early to help my dad review the final preparations. The contractor arrived, and the following ensued:

> Contractor: It looks like you have everything ready to go.
> Dad: I've been ready. Let's get started.
> Contractor: There's just one thing.

Dad: What could that be? You said it looked like we were ready to go.

Contractor: I don't see a hen weigh.

Dad (showing signs of agitation): What's a hen weigh?

Contractor (grinning): About three or four pounds.

I laughed in appreciation at the contractor's "hen weigh" joke. My dad, however, was not amused. Dad was a very patient man, but the contractor had pushed him to the brink by making him wait two weeks and then wasting time with a corny joke.

This anecdote (except for the part about the hen weigh!) pertains to the *permission* rung of the leadership ladder—the place where willing followers join leaders—because permission should be thought of as a permit between two parties. A permit details agreed-upon boundaries governed by laws, regulations, standards, contracts, codes, etc.

A leader has permission to "build" within the boundaries of a permit. However, if the leader chooses to operate outside of those limits, he/she will need to establish a new permit with followers if trust is to be retained.

PERMISSION RUNG LEADERSHIP

In organizations, the authentic story serves as the permit, providing the boundaries that designate wherein a leader can build. (As a reminder, I think of *story* as the combination of *mission* and *vision* working towards the completion of a purpose.) Within those stories, followers willingly agree to build with the leader. But if the leader chooses to operate outside of that story, followers will likely choose to reevaluate—and possibly revoke—their permission. Another way to state this is that if leaders break the trust of followers by operating outside of the authentic story, followers have the right to take back their permission, thus relegating the leader back to the *position* rung with that set of followers. Should this happen, leaders must start over with authentic storytelling and earning trust deposits.

I realize that the concept of *permission* within leadership may seem foreign—and for a good reason. "Permission-based leadership" sounds or feels strange because it *is* strange. Very few people have experienced leaders who view followers as holding the power to choose whether to follow or not. Very few people have experienced leaders who operate using agreed-upon permits that require not only followers but also leaders to be accountable within the leadership relationship.

That said, obtaining permission from followers may still seem awkward to you as a leader, so let's explore the concept of permission in greater detail.

ON MISSION

Permission comes from the Latin word *permittere*, which means "to let go, let loose, give leave." Permission is tied to the idea of submitting or submission. There are, of course, several words in the English language that we hate, and submit and submission are among these. We hate the concept of submitting because we don't understand its meaning; incorrect connotations, such as "weakness" and "power over," are assigned to submitting, turning it into a bad thing.

However, when we break *submission* into its two roots—*sub* and *mission*—we gain the correct perspective on the concept of submitting. *Sub* means "under." My time in the navy was spent in the submarine force—working under water. If we define *mission* as "a general assignment or a pathway to complete a purpose," then we can see how the denotation (actual meaning) of *submission* is a positive one. Submission, or sub-mission, is simply an assignment that takes place under, or within, a larger mission.

The larger mission that a leader articulates is his/her authentic story. When followers grant a permit (permission) to a leader, the leader knows that followers are connecting with the authentic story, believing that their own missions/stories are important subplots to the leader's story. As long as the leader stays witin the boundaries of the story, the follower will likely continue to give the leader permission to lead, and both parties, leader and follower, benefit.

Here Comes the (Empowered) Bride

A good model to facilitate our understanding of this is the concept of marriage. Yes, I know that marriage has been redefined to mean essentially any relationship between two people. And although I may not agree with how the American government defines marriage, that definition has become the law of our land. For simplicity's sake, however, let's apply the old concept of marriage to the idea of gaining permission to lead.

In any relationship, there must be one person who sets the overall mission/story for the relationship, and in traditional marriage, that person has been the husband. During courtship, the male would be expected to communicate to the female his authentic story…of love and what a life together might be. Over time, the couple would see themselves either as fitting together in that story or as moving toward different stories. If they fit together when the time was right, the male would ask the female to place her mission under their overall mission for the marriage—and they would become engaged.

The apostle Paul instructs wives, in the Bible's New Testament book of Ephesians, to submit to their husbands (Ephesians 5:22). That is an empowering statement that our culture has perverted into a restricting one, incorrectly believing that this statement calls for one person to dominate over another. That is because people have a thinking problem; we immediately—and incorrectly— think that submission in marriage is *power over*, in which the stronger person has power over the weaker.

Of course, there are some who would disagree with my "empowering" claim, so let me go a little further on this idea. A follower giving a leader permission to lead is the pathway to empowerment. Don't miss that. Submission is designed to be empowering—because submission provides a follower the freedom of working within someone else's story while simultaneously refining his/her own story. When this happens, *both* the follower and leader begin to deliver on their stories.

A wife submitting to a husband, then, means she permits him to lead while she positions her story under the overall mission and vision of the marriage. As such, the wife can accept from the marriage empowerment—the transfer of power—to accelerate the completion of her story. In this way, the husband and wife are both working on the general story of the marriage while the wife is simultaneously enabled to work on her specific story. As my wife is fond of saying, "A good marriage makes both people better."

Permission Rung Outcomes

Leaders on the *permission* rung gain willing followers, and willing followers are the foundation for effective teams.

Leaders without effective teams cannot descend beyond the *permission* rung of the leadership ladder, yet team building cannot start before reaching the *permission* rung. Why can't you build effective teams as a positional leader? Because building a team requires trust, and positional leaders are those who have yet to earn followers' trust.

This line of thinking resembles that of Patrick Lencioni, an expert on team building. In his book *The Advantage*,[1] Lencioni discusses five steps toward building an effective leadership team. His first three steps are trust, conflict, and commitment.

>> LEADERS ON THE *PERMISSION* RUNG GAIN WILLING FOLLOWERS, AND WILLING FOLLOWERS ARE THE FOUNDATION FOR EFFECTIVE TEAMS.

As we previously discussed, granting trust is an action the follower must initiate for the leader to move down the leadership ladder from the *position* to the *permission* rung. Trust creates a safe place for a follower, and thus, trust is a necessary first step in building teams. When people feel safe, they will bring with them all they have: ideas, creativity, experiences, innovations, and so on. If followers don't bring all they have (if there is no trust), the team will suffer.

The next step is conflict. With a proper understanding of what trust means, this second step might not seem all that strange. When trust exists, people feel invited to deliver what they think is best for the organization to achieve its story—even if what they deliver is disagreement. Teams must be able to vet various, competing approaches to solving problems, with each team member building a case for his/her approach. If teams claim that the whole is greater than the sum of the parts (meaning that *synergy* exists), then the parts need to be allowed to engage in a "healthy" vetting/conflict process! I put "healthy" in quotes because conflict can only be healthy if trust is tangible.

The third step is *commitment*, specifically shared commitment, which is the natural result of a conflict that is built upon trust. When people can be part of the solution, the solution becomes a shared commitment, and the need to obtain "buy-in" becomes unnecessary.

FINAL THOUGHTS

The permission rung of the leadership ladder should be considered a place of honor, of privilege...not a rite of passage. People don't *have to* follow you—I don't care what your title is. If the thought creeps into your head that you "deserve" to lead, banish that idea. Instantly. Regardless of whether people carry your DNA or you sign their paycheck, people still *choose* to follow you.

And their choice to do that, if indeed they do, is humbling... for you, as the leader.

When people are willing to put their trust and confidence in you and the authentic story you tell, you must take that privilege seriously and work tirelessly to deliver on their behalf. Keep in mind that you aren't delivering against the story for you but rather for those who are willing to put some coins in your trust bank.

Again, leadership is not about power but empowerment (as the next chapter discusses in detail). Leading is about empowering those who are willing to follow, transferring authority to them. When authority is transferred, others can start applying their gifting toward the organization's story, augmenting team synergy, and lifting the organization higher than before.

9

FROM PERMISSION TO PRODUCTION:
We Will Be Able

Once a leader has moved to the *permission* rung, meaning that people have chosen to follow because they believe in the authenticity of the leader's story, a leader must take inspired action consistent with that story in order to climb down to the *production* rung of the leadership ladder. A leader's inspired activities will enable a picture of the future to come into clearer focus. A leader who tells an authentic story that inspires action consistent with the story is known as someone who "walks the talk."

Dr. Martin Luther King, Jr. was certainly that kind of leader.

In August 1963, Dr. King delivered his *I Have a Dream...* speech, one of the most powerful speeches in American history. In the first part of the speech, Dr. King repeated the phrase "I have a dream" to connect his authentic story to the inspired actions he was taking. But if he had stopped there, his speech wouldn't have had the impact that it did. His speech continued with:

"This is our hope, and this is the faith that I go back to the South with.

"With this faith, we will be able to hew out of the mountain of despair a stone of hope. With this faith, we will be able

to transform the jangling discords of our nation into a beautiful symphony of brotherhood. With this faith, we will be able
to work together, to pray together, to struggle together, to go
to jail together, to stand up for freedom together, knowing
that we will be free one day."[1]

With this latter portion of his speech, Dr. King empowered
those in attendance and those who would later read his words.
He shifted from the inspirational "I have a dream" phrase to the
empowering words "we will be able" and "together." Please note,
however, that for empowerment to be effective, inspiration must
come first.

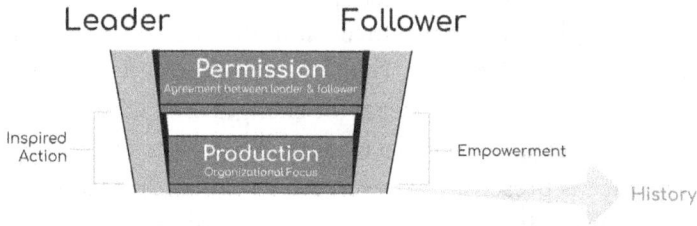

DESCENDING TO THE PRODUCTION RUNG: LEADER'S ROLE

A typical and tough leadership question concerns *how to deliver
consistent actions*. To keep our actions consistent, we try to be
(self-) disciplined, or we try to put motivators in front of us.
However, we seldom have enough discipline or the right motivators to keep our behavior uniform.

Given that, I believe we are asking the wrong question. Instead
of asking how we can deliver *consistent* actions, I believe we
need to be asking how we can deliver *inspired* actions—inspired
actions are what move leaders down to the *production* rung
on the leadership ladder and allow them to have impact there.
Why inspired actions?

To understand the answer, we need to investigate discipline, motivation, and inspiration further.

DISCIPLINE

Discipline is the threat of a negative consequence designed to change or to contain a behavior. This threat can be internal and/or external. Internal discipline is referred to as "self-discipline;" external discipline is applied by someone else when we lack self-discipline.

Typically, discipline produces short-term behavioral change. We certainly see that in the military. If the physical discipline of boot camp were an effective long-term solution, the military wouldn't have any behavioral problems—but it does. Why? Because discipline alone produces short-term behavioral changes.

What makes discipline "bad" is not that it is punitive but rather that it is temporary; behavior changes only while the threat/fear of (a) internal or external stimuli or (b) a severe negative consequence is present. However, once that threat is diminished, once the fear dissipates, or once the severity of the negative consequence goes away, the behavior often reverts to its original form.

For example, the threat of a severe negative consequence could be a health problem. Have you ever considered why many heart attack survivors strictly eat according to the doctor's recommendation for a certain period? Initially, while the survivor's heart attack is fresh in mind, threats of another hospital stay or of sudden death are real and present; hence, discipline is strong. The more time that passes, however, the less frequently a survivor thinks about these threats, and discipline wanes. Again, discipline is temporary and most effective while the fear of external stimuli or severity of a negative consequence is real and present.

MOTIVATION

Motivation differs from discipline in that motivation utilizes a *positive* internal and/or external benefit, or positive reinforcement.

If the positive stimulus exists, the behavior typically conforms or molds to the desired standard. But once the positive stimulus is removed, the behavior modifications/improvements eventually dissipate, and the old behavior returns.

Examples of this phenomenon are many. Some parents pay their children for earning good grades. If these parents continue to fund their kids' activities and bank accounts, most students will work hard enough to make the grades. Some organizations use a bonus program based on a set of metrics geared toward compelling behaviors that organizations believe will improve their overall performance. These metrics may change annually; if they are measurable and achievable, the organization will likely experience the desired behavior. Remove the reward, however, and both organizations and parents will have trouble facilitating the desired outcomes for their employees and students.

Now, motivation is not a bad thing. Motivation can be a catalyst for driving improved performance. The challenge is keeping the motivation relevant and significant. Otherwise, motivation will be ineffective in driving the desired behavior. Exhibit A of this occurrence is the $64 billion[2] weight-loss industry. This industry banks (literally!) on the fact that customers will be motivated for some period, then allow that motivation to deteriorate—only to regain it later. A large portion of consumers of weight-loss products and services do not seem to be looking for a permanent change in behavior but rather for a motivated, moderate-term change; consequently, they keep coming back for the latest weight-loss products.

INSPIRATION

Inspiration is the place we want to be as leaders; it's the place where great organizations live. *Inspire* is a combination in the Latin words for "in" and "breathe." Have you ever stopped to ask yourself what *you're* breathing in? When you breathe in your story and purpose, inspiration will flow out, meaning inspired actions will occur.

Breathing in your story means talking about the story, thinking about the story, making the story like air: life-giving. That's right, the energy (work force) that causes our actions to be inspired comes from the story itself. This makes inspiration superior to discipline and motivation.

Discipline draws its energy from the threat of negative consequence, and motivation draws its energy from the promise of a positive benefit. So with discipline or motivation, we must keep the threat or benefit continually present and relevant if we want to keep our actions aligned with the story. However, we know that threats and benefits cannot be kept ever present or perpetually relevant. And when the energy required to keep our actions aligned with the story fades, trust deteriorates...and we lose permission to lead.

A follow-up question is whether the story—unlike threats and benefits—can generate an infinite amount of energy to keep a leader's actions inspired. The answer is yes...and no. Yes, the story will always generate energy if it is the right story, but, no, sometimes we need a little additional work force or boost to breathe in the story deeply.

For instance, during my days at the power plant, we could add supplemental burners to boost our output at times when the power demand was exceptionally high. What is the supplemental burner to boost a leader's inspiration? Staying connected to the source of the inspiration. Engaging or interacting with the source of your inspiration will provide supplemental energy to help you breathe in the story deeply and thus keep your actions both aligned with the story and inspired!

>> THE ENERGY (WORK FORCE) THAT CAUSES OUR ACTIONS TO BE INSPIRED COMES FROM THE STORY ITSELF.

As leadership is primarily about people, the source of a leader's inspiration *is* people, generally. Specifically, my story is to help people discover the keys to unlock their leadership potential.

Consequently, if I am going to stay inspired, I need to stay connected to people seeking to become better leaders, and I need to study and apply leadership in my own life.

STORY PROBLEMS

When you know your story, you know the general direction of the finish line before you start running the race. Knowing the most efficient route to the finish line, however, is not always clear.

When you struggle (and you will!) to deduce that route, don't stop going forward. You must keep moving—because movement means you've already overcome inertia and thus are better equipped to "course-correct" toward the finish line as it begins to come into focus. As any sailor knows, turning a ship with forward momentum is much easier than steering one that's barely crawling through the water.

Discipline and motivation will keep you moving. Sometimes you need discipline and motivation to simply serve as the spark that keeps your momentum moving ahead as you search for the most efficient route toward your destination, your story. So know that although discipline and motivation are not long-term solutions, they can be effective mechanisms for facilitating short-term progress.

POWER SUPPLY

Some "leaders" fail to recognize that they can't get to the end of the story without followers helping them. Because any organization's story is a shared endeavor (a leader's story must fit together with others' stories), many people—including me—need to be reminded: No leader can arrive at the destination alone. If you find yourself alone as a leader...well, you are simply alone (and not a leader). Isolation, not destiny, is where you are headed.

As a leader, a wonderful way to encourage followers to share your journey is to share your power. Conversely, leaders who do not empower followers will have little or nothing to show for their leadership.

Empowerment is placing power within another. The term *empower* is comprised of the prefix *em-* which means "in" and the word *power*, which means "the ability to act or do." Thus, to empower is to place the ability to act or do within someone else.

To understand how this works, we need to understand the essence of power. And to understand the essence of anything, I default to equations. Consider this one:

Power = Knowledge + Skills + Authority + Attitude

To empower, then, means to place proper knowledge, skills, authority, and attitude within another. In stating this, I am not claiming that a leader is responsible for making followers smarter, more skillful, or attitudinally positive. What I do believe, though, is that a leader is responsible for shaping environments in which followers can make positive strides toward improving their knowledge, skills, and attitudes.

Additionally, prior to offering followers empowerment, a leader must take inspired actions—because when a leader tells an authentic story and then takes actions that are inspired by that story, a physiological change occurs in the people around the leader. Humans are created to be in relationship. That means we have relational chemicals within us, such as serotonin and oxytocin. When those chemicals are released, we want to be a part of whatever caused that release. A leader causes those chemicals to be released through the combination of authentic storytelling and inspired actions. Conversely, if no authentic storytelling and inspired actions occur, a follower might not want to receive the empowerment that a leader offers.

BOXED IN

The empowerment box (Figure 9.1) helps us understand the concept of leaders placing power within followers.

The leader defines the boundaries of the box as related to authority; that is, the leader stipulates the amount and type of authority given to a follower to complete a specific task. Both leaders and followers are then responsible for making sure that followers possess the knowledge, skill, and attitude commensurate with the task for which authority is given. For instance, if a follower is empowered to change the organization's social media presence, he/she should have knowledge of various platforms such as Facebook, Twitter, and Instagram, but knowledge of the company's purchasing processes is not necessary for his/her empowerment to be effective. Likewise, if a follower is empowered to change human resources policies, he/she does not need to possess accounting skills for his/her empowerment to be effective.

Empowerment Box

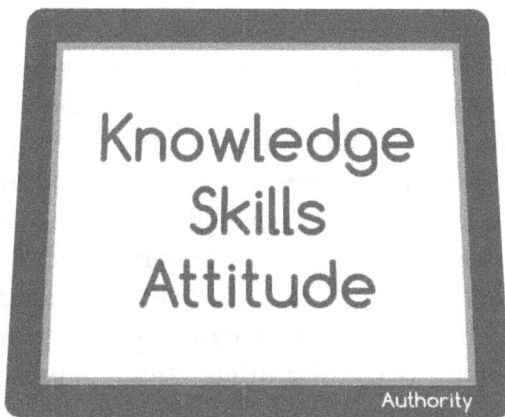

Knowledge
Skills
Attitude

Authority

Figure 9.1 – The Empowerment Box

There is one final point about the empowerment box. Once the box is established (meaning once authority is specified and followers possess the proper knowledge/skills/attitude), followers are "in" the box, and leaders must stay "out." One of the fastest ways to destroy the morale of an organization is for leaders to continually step inside the empowerment box of followers without formal permission, thereby undermining the authority they've given to followers.

POWER CYCLE

Another aspect of empowerment concerns a leader's understanding of who should be empowered. There is an old saying that *absolute power corrupts absolutely*. Given that, the United States Constitution instituted three equal branches of the federal government and allocated most of the power to the state level (whether power is shared in such a manner today is a topic of much debate).

The only way to ensure that power doesn't corrupt *you* is to give it away—to empower others. Leaders need to find and empower those who are not looking for power. Empowering an individual who wants power will likely result in a negative outcome (which is why evaluating the attitude of those we empower is so important).

Why is it bad to empower someone who wants power? People who are seeking to gain power will not pass the empowerment baton but instead will hold it tightly to preserve their position. We see this dynamic all the time: pastors who don't want to empower the church's volunteer staff; politicians who are more concerned with maintaining their powerful office than empowering the people they are elected to serve; and parents who refuse to empower their kids, instead resorting to the "you do what I tell you as long as you live in my house" approach. A leader should look for people who have the capability, knowledge, skills, and attitude to accept a transfer of power and who understand power as the hot rock it is, a rock that will burn if not frequently passed. Such people tend to be committed to the organization's story and more focused on the organizational destination than on their own journeys.

Empowerment only works if people view possessing power as a relay race where the baton of empowerment gets passed from one person to the next. Those who are willing to keep the cycle going are the ones leaders should look to empower. A leader can never be sure how followers will respond when empowered, but putting effort into finding the right followers to empower is always worth a leader's time.

ACCEPTANCE = ACCOUNTABILITY

One last thing for leaders to understand on this topic: Empowerment cannot be forced, and some followers reject the empowerment offered to them. There are numerous reasons for this, but most of these have the same root: fear. Of course, this fear can be alleviated by the leader's (a) ensuring that followers possess the proper knowledge, skills, and attitude and (b) remaining outside of the empowerment box.

Accountability is the other reason followers might reject empowerment. Accountability is often viewed as the person in power demanding answers from a subordinate; therefore, accountability tends to have a negative connotation. If that is indeed how accountability is viewed in your organization, followers will struggle to accept empowerment. Why? Because people don't want to be held to account in a punitive way.

What accountability *should* be is a positive discussion regarding the ability to execute within the empowerment box; this should be a frank, safe, two-way conversation that benefits both leaders and followers. Is this what happens in your organization? If not, (re)defining *accountability* is a good place to start if you want to change the minds of those you want to empower.

Without this positive approach to accountability, followers will feel paralyzed, fearing negative accountability (read: punishment) if things go wrong. Fearful followers progress little—certainly less than the leader desires. Hence, observing limited progress in followers, the leader feels justified in taking back the empowerment, thinking, "I guess I'll just have to do the job myself." Taking back empowerment in this type of situation is equivalent to *fake* empowerment—meaning that, ultimately, the leader doesn't want to empower followers. (The leader is convinced that he/she is the keeper of all knowledge and skill, that he/she has ultimate authority anyway, and that things are always better when he/she works alone.) The root of fake empowerment stems from the imbalance in leadership and management, resulting in an over-managed/under-led organization, as discussed in chapter 3.

DESCENDING TO THE PRODUCTION RUNG: FOLLOWER'S ROLE

On the leadership ladder, *empowerment* is on the follower side rail, because accepting empowerment from leaders requires followers who have skin in the game. That is, empowerment is a matter of mutuality: Both the leader and the follower have a responsibility (and risk!) related to the four components of power (knowledge, skills, authority, attitude). Examining each of these components in greater detail will illustrate this point.

KNOW OR NO

Followers need to possess the knowledge necessary to accept empowerment. (When followers lack knowledge, the leader must supply followers with the opportunity to gain knowledge.)

Of course, followers are not required to be omniscient in the area of their empowerment; they must, however, have a working knowledge, the type of knowledge necessary to know what they don't know. I liken working knowledge to the process of learning to drive a car. Student drivers first learn the rules of the road and are tested on that (book) knowledge before beginning their in-car training. The in-car, experiential training does not result in a new driver mastering all possible driving situations; however, such training should be enough to show drivers how to avoid dangerous situations. That is, such training should provide students with enough knowledge to be good, successful drivers.

If followers do not yet have a working knowledge of a process/situation/relationship/activity/etc., then they should not accept empowerment. Otherwise, followers create an environment wherein failure can be anticipated. Of course, everyone fails at times, but *expecting* failure isn't a healthy organizational environment.

LACK OF SKILL CAN KILL

To properly use power, followers must be able to transfer what is in their heads to their mouths, hands, and feet. But as we're painfully aware, execution—the skilled use of knowledge—is not a given. My driver's ed experience illustrates this point, unfortunately!

When I took driver's ed, the "gaining knowledge" part was easy. I always made good grades and was considered one of the smarter students (*book* smart, that is) in my class. When we moved to the skills phase of our training, however, my book smarts didn't translate into street smarts, as the following anecdote confirms.

David, John, and I had the privilege of driving from 6:00 a.m. to 10:00 a.m. every day for a couple of weeks. One morning, our lesson covered interstate driving. Our teacher was more confident in me than was warranted, and so, to put it kindly, he really wasn't paying attention to what I was doing.

I had the cruise control on and was rapidly approaching a car in front of me that was moving at "2XT" (two times turtle) speed. Of course, I had no idea how to disengage the cruise control. So, I waited until I was mere feet from the car and whipped the wheel hard left, meeting the gravel on the other side of the road, and followed that by jerking the wheel to the right, which (somehow) put us right back in my original lane and in front of the slow-moving car. A results-focused person might say I'd been successful! That wasn't the teacher's perspective, however, as the newspaper flew out of his hands and "#@!*" came out of his mouth. The point of this story is twofold: (a) guardian angels exist, and (b) my skills were not developed enough for me to accept empowerment (to have a driver's license).

A leader must ensure followers have the proper skills before empowering, and if such skills are lacking, the leader needs to supply followers with the opportunity to obtain those skills.

LIEUTENANT ROTH HAS THE CONN

Regarding authority, followers (and leaders) must be clear on (a) who has the authority and (b) the parameters, or limitations, of that authority. Useful to illustrate this point is understanding how authority in the navy is transferred *from* the Commanding Officer (CO) and *among* other officers on watch.

On ships and submarines, the CO has ultimate authority, but he/she can't stay awake and in command around the clock. So, the CO must transfer that authority to others, mainly to the Officer of the Deck (OOD). The OOD stands watch on the bridge or in the control room and is the CO's representative; the CO transfers some authority to the OOD, and when the OOD speaks within that authority, the OOD's orders carry the same weight as the CO's.

The authority transferred to the OOD is not total authority. The CO defines the boundaries of the OOD's authority through written correspondence. After reviewing this correspondence, there is a verbal announcement, such as, "This is Lieutenant Roth, and I have the Conn." This statement makes clear to others on watch who is in control of the ship/sub. If an order needs to be issued that is outside of that boundary of the transferred authority, the OOD seeks out the CO for *authorization to perform*. Without that specific authorization, the OOD cannot issue the order.

This type of clear command doesn't always happen in other organizations. Instead, what is typical is that followers accept authority that is (a) without clear boundaries, (b) not formally transferred, and (c) not well understood by others on the team. This opaque transfer of authority is a recipe for poor execution.

One other thing about naval authority: When the CO wants to take the authority back, there must be another formal transfer. For example, if the CO walks into the control room, he/she can't give an order to the Chief of the Watch (COW) because the authority to give orders was transferred to, and resides with, the OOD. If the CO wants authority back, he/she has to say, "This is the Captain, and I have the Conn." That may sound odd because a captain retains the complete authority that is inherent to his/her position. However, once a captain has transferred authority, he/she must utilize a formal process to take authority back.

What often happens in the boardroom is the CEO or VP of a division doesn't like something and might say, "We are going to stop making red widgets." That may *sound* okay because that CEO or VP has complete authority inherent to his/her position. But that's *not* okay if the decision to make red widgets was under the authority of someone else (a follower). Taking back, or overriding, a follower's authority without a formal process, even if it is "normal" practice, will start to create an organizational culture lacking in trust, initiative, creativity, and cohesiveness (hence the reason the process for transferring authority within the navy is so formal).

RIGHT, OR RIGHTED, ATTITUDE

The final component of power is attitude, and before accepting empowerment, a follower has to (a) examine his/her attitude towards power and (b) allow for an "attitude adjustment" if necessary.

Behavior is an external demonstration of one's attitude. To change behavior, therefore, we must change the way we think, allowing our attitudes to be adjusted, righted.

Followers who want to be empowered but don't have the right attitude should try to change their thinking...and see if there is a corresponding change in their attitude. If there is not an attitude change, a follower should not accept power because empowered followers speak on behalf of the leader. Consequently, an empowered follower with the wrong attitude will undermine the trust a leader has built with other followers.

FINAL THOUGHTS

Pat Tillman was a professional football player for the Arizona Cardinals. He was on the verge of signing a new, large contract when he left the National Football League (NFL) to join the army, to become a ranger. On one level, this made sense. Tillman was part of a team, the Arizona Cardinals, and he left to become part of a different team, the U.S. Army's Rangers. He was using his physical talents and leadership ability in the NFL, and he would use his physical talents and leadership abilities in the army.

However, Tillman made, and was going to make, far more money in the NFL than in the army—thus staying in the NFL seemed much more logical. So why did Tillman leave?

I can't give you a definitive answer, but I believe physiological change occurred in many people in our country (a) when we heard the authentic story of the United States pursuing those who were responsible for the attacks of September 11, 2001, and (b) when we saw the inspired actions numerous others took toward realizing that story. Tillman simply needed to be a part of that.

Inspiration is contagious.

So…are *you* living inspired? Are you living out an authentic story and empowering those around you? Or, for you, is living inspired just an idea(l)—consisting of some encouraging words that would look good on a poster in your conference room or on a piece of driftwood hanging above your fireplace? Without inspired actions, you (and your organization) will require discipline or motivation to achieve short- or mid-term results—results that you will not be able to sustain, relegating the story to a mere wish and the status quo to an unfortunate reality.

10

PRODUCTION RUNG:
History in the Making

In the late 1990s, when I was in the navy and still in relatively good shape, I convinced my wife that she should start running with me. She started slow, but a quarter-mile run/walk soon became a half-mile run/walk; and before long, Sharice was ready for her first 5k race. Being the good husband that I am, I registered us and assured her that we would run together, not compete against one another.

The race started, and that promise vanished from my mind; I took off like a rabbit running from a fox. The problem was that my relatively good shape was not rabbit shape, and with less than a mile until the finish, I realized my wife was right behind me, as I saw her on the other side of the racecourse loop. I then had a decision to make: I could fake pulling my hamstring and let her finish before me because of an "injury," or I could put my head down and run with every ounce of effort I had left.

Well, I picked option #2 and regurgitated my breakfast immediately after passing the finish line, leaving evidence of my... triumph...on my shoes. A short time later, my beautiful wife finished and asked, "Are you proud of yourself?" Even though her tone strongly indicated that her question was rhetorical, I, like an idiot, thought I could provide an acceptable answer. However, the best that came out of my mouth was, "Uh...not really."

I had made a fool of myself—in more ways than one. But thankfully, my foolishness was simply a moment in my history (albeit one I'd like to forget!), and history is simply an event or series of events bound by time. On the leadership ladder, history is the result of climbing down to the *production* rung.

PRODUCTION RUNG LEADERSHIP

We often consider "production" to be a management function—performance against a set metric, such as actual versus budgeted costs. Most of us produce on a regular basis. You might plant a garden and produce tomatoes; you might work in a factory and produce cars; and/or you might open your mouth and produce beautiful music. *Produce* comes from the Latin roots *pro,* which means "forth" and *ducere,* which means "to lead" or "to bring." Produce, then, means "to lead forth or to bring forth."

Production on the leadership ladder means one of two things: bringing forth results that (a) are aligned with the story or (b) that are brought forth by the inspired actions of empowered people. The concept of production may sound simple, but some hazardous behavior is possible on this rung.

Through the first two rungs on the ladder, there is much focus on the story and the destination described by that story. However, when we get to the production rung, our focus shifts from *purpose* to *results.* I'm not saying this shift is a good thing, but it is a real thing...and a dangerous challenge because of the "success" the production rung can project.

A brief reminder about leadership and management illustrates this danger. Leadership and management will work together if we allow, but we often skew our efforts toward management, thus creating an imbalance that limits our personal/organizational output. And if management is going to supersede leadership, the production rung is the place where that will occur...because once you start producing as a leader, you become subject to a cognitive shift toward believing that you must continually maintain and improve on those results. That is, you feel a heavy obligation to increase production.

True, leadership, not management, enabled us to climb down to the *production* rung, but fear of "not producing more" via managing processes can readily replace the reward of leading people. Our dopamine level spikes, and we start wanting to check stuff off *our* list that belongs on someone else's. Translation: Abandoning formal process, we take back the authority we previously transferred to others, and we start depending on discipline and motivation to carry us. I believe this happens because success tends to be a distractor, causing us to take our focus off the story as we revel in our accomplishments.

How do we prevent this cycle from happening to us?

We need to listen…to the right story.

Like children who want to read the same story in the morning, before naptime, and before going to bed, we, as leaders, need to be eager to read (and re-read!) our story. A few chapters at breakfast, another few at lunch, and the final few before bedtime…that's a good approach. Of course, I'm not suggesting that you should get lost in your story all day and thus not work.

But I am stating that when leaders on the *production* rung think and talk too little, too infrequently about the story, their organizations can readily digress from balanced organizations to over-managed/under-led organizations.

LIKE FATHER, LIKE SON

My two boys spent a few summers working at the power plant I managed. My younger son made a statement once that was very accurate but also very hard for many leaders—like me—to accept. He said, "Dad, you are a highly paid cheerleader."

In many respects, he was right, although I didn't feel overpaid! Leaders must keep the story fresh in the minds of those around them by (a) tweaking the picture of the future as it comes into focus and then (b) empowering the heck out of their teams to keep on painting without losing sight of the final picture.

The production rung is where the leadership rubber meets the road, where leadership men and women are separated from leadership boys and girls. What separates these two groups is that leadership adults refrain from reverting to *managing* (controlling) followers to ensure that the desired results are achieved; instead, these leaders empower followers—leading them forth, keeping the vision/story ever present in the hearts and minds of all organizational members.

If you want to be a list-checker-offer, then stay in a management role. Please. Managers play an essential role in all successful organizations!

However, if you want to lead, then upon reaching the *production* rung, you must dig in and drive the story to and through every single employee, from the janitor to the CEO. Lead forth and see what you—collectively—can produce!

PRODUCTION RUNG OUTCOMES

By now, you know that gaining followers and placing power within those followers will move you to the *production* rung of the leadership ladder. And the *production* rung is where you will become a history maker. History is an event or series of events bound by time. The word *history* is often broken into two pieces: "his" and "story." And actually "his-story" is a useful way to frame how we approach history—i.e., a person's producing against a story in such a way that we connect an event to him/her.

For something to be considered historic, two conditions must be in place: (a) the event must be bound by time and (b) something tangible or measurable must have been accomplished. For instance, all of these are historical events/developments: the Kansas City Royals won the 2015 MLB World Series, Alexander Graham Bell invented the telephone, President Bush ordered the invasion of Iraq, and Nelson Mandela ended apartheid in South Africa. The ultimate significance of most historical events requires time to pass and later generations to judge how an event impacted society. But whether "moment in time" events are eventually determined to have positive or negative consequences has no bearing on whether such events are historical.

History is important—so important that we all study it for many years in school. We study local history, state history, national history, and the people who were the catalysts behind historical events. Depending upon where we were born, the details of *what* history we study are different. But the reason *why* we study history is the same.

We study history because it gives us a window into *who* we are and from *where* we came. Additionally, we gain insight into *how* influential people thought and acted. History records the results of the decisions we (on an individual, organizational, and societal level) have made.

In business, history is a *lagging indicator*, a measurement used to evaluate our actions to determine how well actual results matched our expected results. History, as a lagging indicator, provides us with (a) an understanding of how to adjust our course based on actual results and (b) a connection to our origin, both from a geographic and ethnic perspective.

Although there are numerous positive aspects of history, history also comes with its own set of dangers. Many people live "historically," meaning that they feel paralyzed by the events of the past or are afraid of what may lie ahead. Consequently, these people are only comfortable operating (mentally and emotionally) where/when they already know the outcome. You have probably come across such people...who want to talk about *only* the past *all* the time; they are unwilling to discuss what *might be*, preferring to live in the familiarity of what *has been*. This "historical" mindset is locked into the belief that there is very little risk living in the past. Is that where you want to live? Is already-made history enough for you?

HISTORY = LEGACY?

We often (and incorrectly) use *history* and *legacy* interchangeably. For instance, people state that President Obama's "legacy" will be the Affordable Care Act. That bill isn't legacy; it is history—"his-story," an event bound by time that represents a measurable/tangible accomplishment. The word origin of *legacy* is tied to "delegate" or "ambassador," a person who represents another person, entity, or country.

>> FOR SOMETHING TO BE CONSIDERED HISTORIC, TWO CONDITIONS MUST BE IN PLACE: (A) THE EVENT MUST BE BOUND BY TIME AND (B) SOMETHING TANGIBLE OR MEASURABLE MUST HAVE BEEN ACCOMPLISHED.

Since one's history stops when he/she is no longer attached to a specific organization or in a specific job, President Obama is no longer making history as the president of the United States, but his legacy could still be growing. Legacy is harder to identify than history because legacy isn't bound by time...and is not normally quantifiable until long after someone leaves a position.

I'll discuss legacy in more detail in a subsequent chapter.

>> THE PRIMARY REASON FOR EMPOWERING FOLLOWERS IS TO CREATE A MASS OF PEOPLE WHO ARE MOVING IN A SPECIFIC DIRECTION WITH A CERTAIN SPEED.

GAINING MOMENTUM

As I noted in chapter 1, John Maxwell conceptualized the rungs of the leadership ladder, and when Maxwell discusses production, he uses the term *momentum*, because on the production rung is where organizations gain momentum.[1] In physics (and keeping with my "fun with equations" [ahem] theme), we learn that:

$$Momentum = Mass * Velocity$$

In organizations, mass can be considered a group of empowered people. Velocity, of course, represents speed and direction. Momentum, then, is a group of empowered people moving in a specific direction with a certain speed. The direction—the path toward the destination—is described by the story.

Momentum occurs on the *production* rung of the leadership ladder because leaders (a) have told an authentic story and (b) have empowered followers. Typically, followers are not empowered because they can perform a function better than a leader—they often can't. Rather, the primary reason for empowering followers is to create a mass of people who are moving in a specific direction with a certain speed.

FINAL THOUGHTS

Producing is about gaining organizational momentum, a mass of empowered people moving together, in the same direction with the same speed. Producing is good because it indicates there is progress within the story, that the destination is coming into clearer view. Producing makes history because producing creates a series of events bound by time. History can be good or bad, but the one definitive thing about history is that it stops when you stop; because of this, your climb down the leadership ladder needs to go beyond the *production* rung.

Ron Popeil was a history maker as an inventor and a memorable infomercial marketer. Popeil developed a cooking device called the Showtime Rotisserie, and he promoted the rotisserie using the phrase "Set it and forget it!" This clever marketing phrase helped Popeil to sell a lot of rotisseries. However, leaders who practice "set it and forget it"—i.e., those who set their focus on producing and neglect to move beyond that stage—will discover their actual influence is far less than their potential influence.

Leaders live forward. So keep moving down the ladder, working toward the *people development* rung, where you have the opportunity to create a legacy.

11

FROM PRODUCTION TO
PEOPLE DEVELOPMENT:
Apples and Stars Both Fall

Bobby Knight and Peyton Manning are two sports figures popular in Indiana, but the character of only one of these men merits mentioning here. (If you were expecting me to comment on Mr. Manning, you'll have to wait a little longer for that!)

My father taught college with Bobby Knight's stepbrother, so Dad was permitted to watch an Indiana Hoosiers basketball practice that was closed to the public. During the practice, Coach Knight was unhappy with what was happening and started using some very colorful language directed at Steve Alford, who was then Indiana University's star player. Knight eventually kicked Alford out of practice. After practice, Knight came over to Dad and his colleague and asked what they thought of practice. Did I forget to mention that Dad and Knight's stepbrother taught at a Christian college!? As they struggled to answer him, Knight asked another question, "Did you think you were coming to a prayer meeting?"

Coach Knight had 902 wins in forty-two years of coaching. He was quite productive. But he also had problems due to his character. Ultimately, issues with his character forced him to leave Indiana for Texas Tech University after twenty-nine seasons.

Look, I grew up in Indiana and loved Bobby Knight. During his tenure as the Hoosiers coach, he won three national titles, eleven conference titles, and made twenty-four NCAA tournament appearances.

To be certain, Bobby Knight was a history maker.

But the fact is that Knight's infamous temper compelled Indiana University to end Knight's history as its coach sooner than he would have liked.

As I wrote in the previous chapter, history consists of events bound by time. Thus, to escape or to outlast history, to live on beyond our time, we must produce something more than an event or outcome. And to do *that*, we must jettison the "producing" mindset altogether…and take on an "investing" one.

"In what should we invest?" is the right question…almost. The right question is actually, "In whom should we invest?"

"People," is the answer.

Because people *are* the answer.

A leader who invests in and develops others will live on beyond his/her departure; that leader's legacy will endure.

Back to Coach Knight: He certainly developed people, as some of his assistants and former players went on to become successful head coaches, too. However, did he develop people like he could or should have…and, in doing so, create the environment for his legacy to grow?

This is critical to consider, for whether we believe questions about what we *could/should* have done as leaders are fair, they will be asked of us, nonetheless.

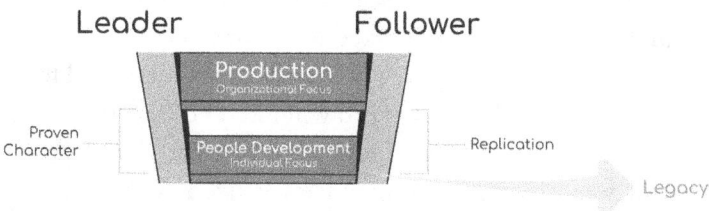

DESCENDING TO THE PEOPLE DEVELOPMENT RUNG: LEADER'S ROLE

Climbing down to the *people development* rung is all about a leader demonstrating character—proven character. Now, what is one's character all about?

The word *character* comes from the idea of something being fixed, etched, meaning that character does not change with changes to the environment. Character, then, is well portrayed by a statue. Take, for instance, the Statue of Liberty; she is the same every day of the week, every week of the year. She is the same during stormy and sunny weather; she perseveres through heat waves and blizzards; she withstands all conditions without changing—that's what any statue is designed to do.

People want to be developed by someone who has character, someone who remains true regardless of the situation. People want a leader with character that's worthy of being emulated, a leader who has integrity—one who *integrates* everything he/she does, rather than acting one way at work and another way at home. Isn't that true for you? Do you gravitate toward people who cheat the system or say whatever is expedient to close a deal? Most people do not. Most people are looking for their leader to be a person whom they aspire to be like.

But the leader's responsibility in moving to the *people development* rung isn't merely demonstrating character but rather proven character.

Because *proven* means "tested, revealed over time" and *character* means "fixed and immovable," the phrase *proven character* may at first seem like an oxymoron. For how can something that is revealed over time also be fixed and immovable?

Here's how. What is fixed, immovable is *your* standard for character. Now, this standard may (and will likely) differ from someone else's standard, which is fine. However, once you define that standard, how you measure your character is fixed. With each one of your decisions and actions, you prove—reveal over time to yourself and to others—how closely your life matches this fixed standard.

A COSTLY, RISKY ENTERPRISE

Developing great character comes at a great cost. "Sweat equity" is the main investment one must make as he/she labors to create a foundation from which great character can be formed. How is character formed? Through stress testing. Stress testing is a simulation technique often used in the banking industry. Stress testing is also used on asset and liability portfolios to determine their reactions to different financial situations. Additionally, stress tests are used to gauge how certain stressors will affect a company, industry, or specific portfolio.[1]

Stress testing of your character acts the same way: You find yourself in various situations or stressors and your action, inaction, or reaction either proves or disproves your character. Additionally, the impact of your action, inaction, or reaction is felt by your organization or family. Developing character is not a new concept, yet people tend to discount the merit of stress testing by saying things like "no one is perfect" or "we are all sinners." Those statements (mindsets) are simply cop-outs, attempts to avoid the fact that great character can be developed if you are willing to put in the effort.

Why does character matter? If you are a person of destiny, one who believes you have a divine purpose that you're expected to accomplish, then character matters very much—because your purpose is part of a bigger puzzle. Thus, until your piece of the puzzle is in place, the puzzle pieces of others whom you're developing won't fit properly. And if others' pieces don't fit together well, the puzzle is incomplete.

>> YOU FIND YOURSELF IN VARIOUS SITUATIONS OR STRESSORS, AND YOUR ACTION, INACTION, OR REACTION EITHER PROVES OR DISPROVES YOUR CHARACTER.

Being intentional about developing others is neither easy nor without risk. Not easy because people are...people. Not without risk because you are required to put your character on display. Constantly. And in doing this, you will be exposed if your character is weak.

Because developing people requires transparency, allowing others unfettered access to who you are and how you think, many people are unwilling to undertake the endeavor; instead, they remain content with *producing* (products, profits, experiences, events, etc.). Please know that my purpose here is not to criticize "producers." I recognize that each of us must make the decision to risk transparency, and such a decision is not easy.

However, my purpose is to challenge us all to strengthen our character to the point where we become comfortable with being transparent. For we really can't be in the business of helping others develop *their* character if we don't first let them explore ours.

SEEING IS BELIEVING

Above, I described *character* by using the meaning of its root word. Another helpful way to gain understanding is to examine one's character from a practical standpoint—how one's character is visible in everyday life.

We have all witnessed poor character. A boss who is clearly bending the rules; an athlete purposefully taking a banned substance; politicians using power to ensure preferential personal benefit or treatment.

Yet although we have a vivid picture of what bad character looks like, this picture isn't always enough to help us understand good character.

The good is often hard to see because one's character is like a seed that remains dormant inside…until it is planted in the right environment. That same seed planted in the wrong environment will never develop. For instance, if you plant an apple seed in the desert, what do you get? You get desert. However, if you plant and nurture that apple seed in parts of Washington state or western Michigan, the result will eventually be a full-grown tree with many apples.

So, keep in mind that character is not a gift or a talent, something you either have or you don't. No, character is something we all possess, something that develops over time through good and bad decisions, right and wrong behaviors, and reactions or responses to opportunities and disappointments. Great leaders work every day to develop character—to deepen their connection to whom they were created to be, thus enabling their character to be fixed and immovable regardless of the environment or people around them. Your character has nothing to do with what you produce. Consequently, character is not part of the production rung of the leadership ladder, but character is a required attribute to move *off* the production rung.

A tangible example of how character is separate from production occurred after Super Bowl XLVIII when the Seattle Seahawks' cornerback, Richard Sherman, tweeted this regarding the Denver Broncos' quarterback, Peyton Manning:

"Peyton is the classiest person/player I have ever met! I could learn so much from him! Thank you for being a great Competitor and person" – Tweet from Richard Sherman February 3, 2014. (@RSherman_25)[2]

The Seahawks had just defeated Manning's team by a score of 43-8. Until then, Sherman had been known for post-game comments touting how he was the best cornerback in professional football. However, his tweet in 2014 demonstrated that he understood something that sports and news "talking heads" often miss: that legacy is about character, not about performance.

Let me rephrase that: Legacy is not something you achieve by winning multiple championships or MVP awards; instead, legacy is something that takes root over time as your character shines through trials and successes.

Manning, one of the best quarterbacks ever, played terribly in Super Bowl XLVIII. Despite that, Manning (no doubt disappointed not only by the loss but also by the *nature* of the loss) sought out Sherman, who was on crutches due to an injury sustained during the game, because Manning wanted to express his concern for Sherman's wellbeing following the injury.

Both Manning's gesture and Sherman's tweet stood in stark contrast to the media chatter about how Manning's legacy was tarnished by the Broncos' loss. If those media members truly understood leadership and climbing down, however, they might have recognized that Manning's legacy was enhanced through the loss because his character had been stress-tested and he had weathered the storm.

FOR AN INSIDE LOOK, LOOK INSIDE

So far, I've discussed two ways we can view character: through etymology (word origin) and observation (of others).

But there is a third way to view character, without which our understanding of character is incomplete. That way is through introspection.

In other words, to fully understand character, we need to understand ourselves fully. So...who are you? Who am I? Who are we?

Genesis, the first book in the Bible, provides us the answers. There, we learn that God created humans in His "image" and "likeness." That we are created in God's image means that we are imbued with His qualities; that we are created in His likeness means we can emulate Him. Of course, this does not mean we *are* God or that we can function *as* God—but our image and functionality are *like* His. We resemble Him.

Genesis also states that God created us male and female, encasing His image and likeness within a body formed from dirt. (This creative act is the source of our word "human" or "humus man," with "humus" meaning *dirt*.[1]) In other words, God created a spirit that possesses His character and functioning and then clothed that spirit in a dirt suit, humus.

The Bible's book of Ephesians lists the fruit of the Spirit: God's Spirit. In other words, this list of qualities describes what the character of God is—and thus what our character should be: love, joy, peace, longsuffering (perseverance), kindness, goodness (integrity), faithfulness (conviction), gentleness (humility), and self-control. Pretty good list. I'm sure that demonstrating these qualities will draw others toward us, allowing us to be a participant in the development of others.

But might this list of character traits be too good, perhaps? Might you think that these qualities are much more *aspirational* than *achievable*?

Let me assure you that we *can* experience this kind of fruit if we so desire—because we were created to bear these qualities. In other words, the seeds of that "good character fruit" have already been planted within us.

What causes those seeds to sprout?

Life. The words we speak, the actions we take, and the information we consume. Our character is often developed in private but always displayed in public. You might think that you can be a "butthead" at home and be a saint in public, but you *will* be exposed, eventually. Our character can't be hidden indefinitely, and why should it be? We want our character—what is true and proven about us—to be on display, so we can impact future generations long after we are gone.

The world needs people of character, and we are not producing them very quickly. Do you want to be a difference maker, a world changer? Become a person of character (today!).

DESCENDING TO THE PEOPLE DEVELOPMENT RUNG: FOLLOWER'S ROLE

The corresponding action required by the followers to climb down to the *people development* rung is *replication*. What does a follower replicate? What they see and hear—the actions and words of the leader.

Simply put, replication is one person behaving similarly in form and function to another person or thing.

We witness replication all around us: a new employee replicating a CEO's words, a tee-ball player replicating a coach's baseball swing, and a concert goer replicating the vibrato of the performer on stage. What do all these examples have in common?

They're all examples of replicating an outward function without necessarily understanding the "why"; that is, these are examples of copying a behavior irrespective of whether one understands the thinking that drives that behavior. We live in a replicate-first, understand-second world; we typically mimic others' words and behaviors prior to knowing and evaluating what thought processes drive those words and behaviors.

While on active duty with the navy, I thought some processes were nonsensical. One such process in place on my first submarine was being told to write my own performance evaluation for my superior to review and to approve—and by doing this, I'd position myself to receive a performance award. How ridiculous is that?

My youngest son is now in the marine corps. He has called me several times to express his frustration with nonsensical processes in the Marines, one of which is the selection process for duty station assignments. When he called to discuss his frustrations, he was saying similar things and acting in a similar way to what I had twenty-five years earlier. In other words, he was replicating my words in actions in railing against some of the inefficiencies in the military. Now, he isn't me, and he isn't in the navy. Additionally, he might not understand the reasons why I fought against military inefficiencies; but he certainly did hear me often talk nonsensical processes, and he did frequently witness my frustration with organizational inefficiencies. So, that he's expressing similar frustrations about nonsensical processes is not surprising (and also makes me proud)!

NATURALLY MESSY

Replication is a natural process; everyone has gone through replication as a baby, learning to walk and talk by mimicking parents, siblings, and/or caregivers. Similarly, in organizations replication building is a process where the follower starts to function more and more like the leader by mimicking the leader. Replication, though, is not meant to produce "robot followers" or clones of the leader. Rather, followers who replicate a leader behave *similarly to* the leader in form and function. In the same way, an aftermarket car part isn't identical to a factory part, but an aftermarket part is a replica, behaving like the factory part in form and function.

And replication will be messy. There will be times when followers have to pick themselves up after failed action or have to apologize after words intended to encourage a coworker actually demoralizes him/her. Replication should be considered a "learning opportunity" and should begin in a controlled environment wherein the consequences are small. We should not expect decisions followers make and outcomes of their actions to have the same results as the decisions and actions of leaders, initially, just like we'd not expect a high school baseball player to hit a home run by replicating Mike Trout's swing for the first time.

>> REPLICATION ISN'T BEING ROBOTIC—FUNCTIONING EXACTLY LIKE SOMEONE ELSE—BUT RATHER BEHAVING *SIMILARLY TO* SOMEONE ELSE, IN FORM AND FUNCTION.

STORIES TELL THE WHOLE STORY

Throughout this book, I've used some examples from the Bible to illustrate points, and I've mainly done this because the central character of the New Testament, Jesus, was an extraordinary leader who climbed down with His followers. After first earning their trust, Jesus next empowered His closest followers, His twelve disciples, to heal a variety of sicknesses and diseases. This empowerment indicated that momentum was growing through a mass of empowered people moving together. Next, the disciples began replicating Jesus, metamorphosing from outward performance, (healing others) to an inward understanding of why healing was occurring.

In one instance, the disciples were unable to cast out a spirit from a boy who was being tormented. But when Jesus arrived, He removed the spirit from the boy. The disciples' inability to heal the boy puzzled them because they had previously succeeded in replicating Jesus by healing others. So, the disciples asked Jesus why they were unable to mimic His actions in that instance, and their questioning indicated their desire to be developed by Jesus.

That's right, curiosity is necessary for people development. If followers do not want to know what is driving the words and actions of the leader, then followers really don't want to *be* like the leader—they merely want to *do* like the leader. But curiosity shows that followers want to know *why*, that they want to go beyond replication and toward transformation, the metamorphosis that occurs on the *people development* rung of the leadership ladder.

FINAL THOUGHTS

Proven character is behavior that is fixed and immovable regardless of the environment, the stress of events, and the pressure to succeed. Proven character is often developed in private—through the relationships we keep, the information we read, and material we view—and displayed in public when we make decisions... often through hard decisions that might have financial or personal ramifications. This public display is what attracts or repels people and is the price of admission if you want to be a people developer.

More than forty former coaches and players under Bobby Knight have gone on to be head men's basketball coaches—the most notable being Mike Krzyzewski, who has more wins than any other Division I men's coach. Does that mean that Knight left a legacy? Not necessarily. Legacy is not learning how to produce from someone; as we have seen, producing results is history, whereas legacy is about people behaving similarly in form and function to someone else. True, Mike Krzyzewski is a tough coach, like Bobby Knight was, but Krzyzewski's character seems not to replicate Knight's.

Replication can be a very challenging process, for both leaders and followers, in part because followers are not (yet) privy to the thinking behind the leader's speech and actions that they're replicating. However, replication has tremendous upside, as replicating is the pathway to people development, and people development is the precursor of legacy.

12

PEOPLE DEVELOPMENT RUNG:
Plowing and Scattering

In December 2018, Urban Meyer held a press conference to discuss his retirement from a long and distinguished career as head coach in college football. At the conference, Meyer was asked if off-the-field issues would impact his legacy, to which he responded: "So the legacy is—you can only control so much. And I can lie to you and say that's not important to me. Any human being, that's important to you. And people will have their opinions. And just do the best to do things the right way."[1]

Later in the conference, a different reporter asked Meyer what he hoped his legacy would look like, and Meyer said: "I hope it's the truth...I talk about the incredible experience you have at a place like Ohio State, and if you act right, do right, you'll have a job. I—we—guarantee that. I hope that's our legacy."

Often when a notable person leaves the job for which they are known, his/her legacy is discussed extensively. That was true for Urban Meyer. Numerous sports journalists addressed Meyer's legacy on the airwaves and in print, including Bill Bender, in an article for MSN.com.

"On the brink of termination and disgrace, Meyer recovered to lead Ohio State and coach his final game at the most-hallowed place for a Big Ten school [the 2019 Rose Bowl]. This is another legacy game for Meyer, and if his track record has shown anything, the Buckeyes will probably send their coach out with a win against 10-3 Washington."[2]

What is a "legacy game," exactly? That is, can a game be a legacy?

No. At least, not if one understands that legacy is about relationships; it is not about records.

Linda Ellis understood this. In 1996, while working for a large corporation, she wrote a poem about legacy entitled *The Dash*.

On her website, Ellis notes, "*The Dash* has truly affected millions. I may not be able to change the world with these words, but I have certainly been able to influence a portion of it."[3]

"Change the world"…words that have been uttered before. Words that people discount as wishful but not practical. Words that most of us believe are not worth more than a passing thought. Maybe what Linda Ellis expressed is what you feel: *I may not be able to change the world.*

But…why not? Who says you can't change the world?

What if *change your world* simply meant to have an impact that is larger than you or to significantly impact a group of people? Could you be a world changer then?

PEOPLE DEVELOPMENT RUNG LEADERSHIP

Essential to people development are two things: potential of followers and transparency of leaders. People development is about (a) understanding and activating the untapped capacity of a follower and (b) opening yourself up as a leader so that a follower can understand how you think.

OPEN…FOR BUSINESS

Followers on the *production* rung only replicated what they saw, heard, and observed, but now, on the *people development* rung, followers need to gain insight on the thinking that drives the leader's thoughts and behaviors.

That, of course, is where transparency comes in.

You can't develop a follower at an arm's length; rather, you must be willing to unlock and unzip your thinking to allow the follower to see what's inside your brain. Both the good and the bad. In other words, don't simply be vulnerable (in allowing access to your thought processes); be authentically vulnerable. Followers already know you're not perfect in your actions—thus they know you cannot be perfect in your thoughts. So don't pretend to be.

In order to really understand what makes you "go" as a leader, followers need the complete picture. So, if you refrain from sharing "you" in whole, then followers' development will only occur in part—they will resort to simply mimicking your action instead of going beyond this, toward applying your thinking in situations unique to them.

Transparency is a word that is used frequently but displayed rarely. So I challenge you to be different, to be courageous enough to be real, to be open with followers. Transparency will not diminish your ability to lead; rather, transparency will enhance a follower's ability to lead.

DEVELOPING NEWS

As a general truth, people are important to any business, family, church, team, club, etc. Why then do we spend so little time, effort, and resources on people development? I believe the answer to this, in part, has to do with (a) our lack of understanding of what people development looks like and (b) the difficulty of developing people.

People management is not equivalent to people development. Don't miss this! People management deals with the current situation, current issues, and current performance. People development deals with potential—a person's future, not a person's present.

Many organizations require performance reviews at defined frequencies. Whether or not you see value in these, many reviews exclusively concern performance management, a horizontal comparison between an individual and a standard (or their peers).

This is problematic because reviews of this nature lack a vertical assessment: a comparison of the current level of performance against future potential. This vertical comparison is *development*, whereas the horizontal comparison is simply *management*.

>> PEOPLE MANAGEMENT IS NOT EQUIVALENT TO PEOPLE DEVELOPMENT. PEOPLE MANAGEMENT DEALS WITH THE CURRENT SITUATION, CURRENT ISSUES, AND CURRENT PERFORMANCE. PEOPLE DEVELOPMENT DEALS WITH POTENTIAL—A PERSON'S FUTURE, NOT A PERSON'S PRESENT.

In the same vein, organizations look to "develop" people by scheduling training and increasing their responsibility toward allowing people to make bigger and more important decisions. But are those things *development*? Yes…if development means "to measure one against the standard of others in similar positions." However, I already challenged that definition and believe true development is not measured by comparing Peter against Paul but rather by comparing Peter against Peter's potential.

People have enormous talents that remain only partially developed because organizations focus on individuals' performance, not their potential. Focusing on potential requires purpose-driven thinking, whereas focusing on performance is results-based thinking. In other words, comparing people based on their performance instead of potential is much easier…but in doing so, in taking the easy way out, organizations are susceptible to neglecting the potential that could transform.

POTENTIAL: NEXT STEPS

Let's pretend for a minute that you push the "I believe you" button and agree that the traditional way of measuring the development of others is incorrect. What now? How do you understand the raw potential of your team and then work toward maximizing that potential?

I submit to you that if analyzing and augmenting potential were easy, you would already be performing these functions. However, performing these functions is difficult, requiring leaders who are willing to spend inordinate amounts of time with their team. But investing such time isn't practical, because you have a job to do as well!

This realization—concerning the abundance of time required to develop people properly—is an important one. And the ramification is this: People development cannot start in earnest until one is on the fourth rung of the leadership ladder.

Why?

Because if your organization is unbalanced (if it is over-managed/under-led), then you will simply not have enough hours in the day to develop people.

So, the first step in maximizing others' potential is to balance your organization so that you will have extra time to invest in each member of your team.

The second step is to help those on your team identify their gifts, their natural talents—those activities in which they would participate even if they weren't being paid. That takes observation, allowing people to "try" things and maybe take on different jobs. Often, other people see your gifts before you see them because what you are good at comes easy, seems natural, and therefore does not seem special. A leader can and should help followers recognize their strengths and encourage their development in their areas of gifting.

The third step, once we have helped connect people with their gifts and talents, is to move others into a position that allows them to be used. "First who, then what" comes from Jim Collins, author of *Good to Great.*[2] Collins believes the right people in the right seats on the bus will take the bus where it needs to go without tremendous management oversight. Why might a leader struggle with putting people in positions that will allow people to maximize their capabilities? Fear, insecurity, risk, wrong thinking, organizational process, etc. There are many reasons; none of them good but all of them real! People development is hard, but "hard" isn't a reason to avoid it. Do you want to really matter as a leader? Be a people developer. There isn't much competition on that rung of the ladder!

PEOPLE DEVELOPMENT RUNG OUTCOMES

Here again, we realize an important difference between history and legacy. The past won't change the future. Your history won't change the world, in that other events, others' histories will someday eclipse yours. Take the *I Have a Dream* speech. Did that event—the making of the speech in 1963—change the world? No. Did the legacy of Martin Luther King, Jr.? Yes.

As noted, legacy and history are not the same; one is bound by events in time, the other is not; one is restricted to your years on earth, the other is not; one is written about in textbooks, the other lives on through people.

>> LEGACY INVOLVES CREATING AN ENVIRONMENT *DURING* OUR DASH THAT ALLOWS US TO LIVE *BEYOND* OUR DASH.

Linda Ellis put 212 words together that were meant to be together, and the resultant impact on people has been significant. But if our "dash" is merely our history, our life won't have the same impact as the poem.

The way our life has an impact, the way our dash lives beyond the years that bracket it, is through legacy. Legacy involves creating an environment *during* our dash that allows us to live *beyond* our dash; in other words, legacy is about changing our world today and tomorrow—and continuing to do so for future generations. For example, Martin Luther King, Jr.'s impact is felt today, not because of his history but because of the legacy he left for you and me.

Do we simply make a verbal claim and wish our legacy into existence? Do we merely spend time with people of significance and legacy rubs off on us? Is legacy automatically built into the last name we receive at birth?

None of those are correct, of course. Nonetheless, legacy is not hard to understand…it's simply hard to execute…because it is about people development.

OFFICE OF THE AMBASSADOR

Above I described a way of looking at people development that is both horizontal and vertical. Horizontal is the traditional way, comparing one's performance to a standard or that of their peers. Vertical people development is about comparing one to his/her potential. This type of development is hard and requires real effort, but is it worth the effort? That is, if a leader produces and makes *history*, does *legacy*—people development—matter?

Well…yes. (Otherwise I wouldn't have asked the question, right!?)

As I have noted previously, *legacy* comes from a word that means "ambassador." A country sends ambassadors around the world to formally represent and advance its interests. Ambassadors carry the message of their home country's government. They live in and integrate into foreign nations so that they build relationships with foreign governments—and such relationships allow ambassadors to be trusted and to have influence.

Ambassadors do not transmit their messages or modify the messages of their country; rather, ambassadors carry the messages issued from their home country's head of state or state department.

What ambassadors represent, then, is *legacy*. They carry forward the story, the desires, the mindsets, the values of "another" (individual or branch of government) by incorporating such story, desires, and values into their original and unique style for the ambassador role. Ambassadors don't abandon who they are, as that would make their message unreliable and their authenticity questionable. Instead, ambassadors carry the message in their own, unique way, not changing the message but delivering it using their authentic self. This is a vital point: Legacy isn't about creating identical images but rather about continuing to further a message in unique and authentic ways. Even the Creator didn't create humans identical to Him but rather in His image and likeness, with the capability of functioning similarly.

Many people spend their lives producing and have tremendous success. What many fail to fully appreciate, though, is that they cannot live forever, and their production is bound by the time that they reside on planet earth. Without facilitating an environment wherein their legacy can grow, they have effectively reduced their impact to the timeframe for which they are alive. That shouldn't be our goal; we should seek a longer-term impact. We should strive to leave a legacy—people who continue to impact others in the same way we have impacted them; this is how we extend our impact beyond our sphere of influence and beyond our lifetime.

I've said several times in this book that John Maxwell shaped much of my leadership thinking, and the *Climbing Down* leadership model uses his stages as the rungs on the leadership ladder. I hope that I can take Maxwell's ideas and enhance them, use them in ways he hasn't, and impact even more people along the way. I want to continue and grow his legacy today, tomorrow, and in the future. What else do I hope? That someone comes behind me and embraces then enhances my ideas, growing my legacy and Maxwell's!

OFFICE OF THE PARENT

Most of us understand legacy at some level because we refer to our children as our "legacy." Our children indeed can be our legacy and thinking of them as such indicates we have a basic understanding of legacy. However, our kids will only be a product, something we have produced as part of our history, if we don't focus our efforts on creating an environment wherein our children have some purpose for which to serve as ambassadors.

Think of it this way: What would you want your kids to carry on, regarding influence, after you die? Do you want them to talk to their kids the way you talk to them? Do you want them to treat their spouse the way you treat yours? These types of things are major, *life* considerations! We must start thinking about the "every day" in a much bigger way. Small thinking will produce small results, whereas big thinking creates an environment wherein big things can occur.

Now, much of what I've written in this book are lessons I've learned by trial and error—with an emphasis on *error*. For instance, I didn't appropriately speak to my kids during some of their formative years, my attitude was sometimes bad, and I wasn't the least bit interested in a discussion of legacy. I could be a "butthead" to use one of my favorite terms. Yes, you read that correctly: Brian equaled *butthead* back in the day.

Fortunately, I surrounded myself with some people who were interested in my legacy and helped me understand this idea of leaving ambassadors behind. Consequently, I was able to change my thinking, and following that change, I made a significant shift in attitude and behavior. It's never too late! Don't miss this point—you are *not* too late to begin forming the environment wherein your legacy can grow. I don't care where you are in life (if you are reading this, I assume you are still breathing). If you have breath, you can start forming the environment wherein legacy can grow and develop, the environment wherein the replication of your message and character can begin.

Note the use of the verb "can" in the previous sentence... indicating that legacy is not automatic. Legacy is about the leader plowing the ground and scattering the seed, thus establishing the conditions where growth is possible. However, the follower must water the seed for growth to occur—otherwise, the seeds of the leader's legacy will lie dormant.

SPIN CYCLE

So...does this means that you can (only) influence your environment, but you can't control your legacy?

Correct, you *can't,* as in "cannot."

Wait. What? No. C'mon—am I claiming that you can't control your legacy?

I am, because, as has already been stated, living out a legacy means living as an ambassador. Ambassadors do not carry—do not control—their own message but rather carry the message of the person, or the branch of government, leading their home country.

But don't fret: Being unable to control our legacy does not mean we cannot grow it.

To illustrate this point, let me again use the example of Jesus, the main character in the New Testament of the Bible. Jesus had many followers, but twelve of them spent much time with him. Jesus was a people developer because He knew His time on earth was short; thus, His impact would be limited unless people carried on His message in their unique and authentic ways (for instance, Peter's approach was different from John's, whose approach was different from Barnabas'). Still, Jesus didn't create His legacy but rather created the environment that allowed His legacy to grow after he was gone.

How did Jesus do this? Like a potter crafts clay. Like a *good* potter crafts clay, that is.

I was a potter once, for a semester. I took a college pottery class, and in this class we would take clay, place it on the potter's wheel, add some water, and, with the motion of the wheel and gentle pressure, form a pot, a cup, or, in my case, an unrecognizable item that was more of a "pup"—a cross between a pot and a cup! (In my defense, I was a physics major, so pottery wasn't exactly in my…wheelhouse!)

Of course, even the best potters in the class didn't throw a lump of clay on the wheel and return a pot, cup, or pup without several cycles of water, pressure, and motion. That cycle or circuit of water, pressure, and motion created the environment for a pot or cup to take shape. But does that cycle *guarantee* a pot or cup would be formed? Ask my college art professor, Craig Moore, and he'd laugh at that question!

Creating the legacy environment is like forming pottery—a cycle of numerous processes. In shaping a legacy environment, a leader must (a) pour his/her character, message, experiences, and values into followers; (b) assist followers in erasing any part of the hard drive in their heads that might be restraining their development; (c) provide followers with input in crafting their story so that it authentically communicates the destination where their gifts and purpose intersect; and (d) dust off, wind up, and send out followers again when things didn't go as hoped or planned the first time.

>> FOLLOWERS HAVE A CHOICE. THEY CAN CHOOSE TO REJECT THE CYCLE, THE LEGACY ENVIRONMENT. THEY CAN CHOOSE TO GO A DIFFERENT DIRECTION AND NOT CARRY ON THE LEADER'S CHARACTER, VALUES, AND MESSAGE.

This cycle continues and adjusts as followers grow. But remember…followers have a choice. They can choose to reject the cycle, the legacy environment. They can choose to go a different direction and not carry on the leader's character, values, and message. They can choose to neglect their story and not develop their gifts or use them to assist others. Should this occur, the followers would not be considered the leader's legacy.

One last point about Jesus and His twelve disciples. Did each of them become His legacy? No, one of them betrayed Him, turning Him over to the local authorities who were looking for Him. Consequently, even the leader who was the greatest of all time didn't score 100% in the legacy department—because all the leader can do is create the environment for his/her legacy to grow, not grow their legacy. Fair? Fairness isn't the issue. The real issue is whether you want to be a history maker or legacy leaver. This choice is one we all must make or allow it to be made for us.

I wasn't a very good potter in college—unable to create an environment wherein a pot, cup, or bowl could be shaped. However, by (a) telling an authentic story and gaining trust, (b) taking inspired actions and empowering those around me so that we produce for the organization, and (c) proving my character through successes and failures, I can create an environment where the "clay" of others can be shaped on the potter's wheel of life.

And with careful pressure, gently molding others' character, adding a little water to soften their clay or wash them off when they fail, and celebrating when they become the "cups" someone else can drink from, my legacy environment will have completed one more cycle.

FINAL THOUGHTS

History makers are great people who are forever remembered for the time they lived and the events they orchestrated. Legacy leavers are remembered forever because they live in the daily interactions of those they impacted.

History makers are recorded and studied. Legacy leavers are often unknown to the people they impact because legacy leavers are ambassadors whose proven character becomes the foundation of replication in others.

If you want to be *known*, attempt to make history. If you want to leave the world a better place than you found it, work toward establishing an environment where your legacy can grow. Stay focused on your purpose and let your inspiration guide you. In doing this, you will become famous…maybe not *world* famous but certainly famous within *someone's* world.

To end this chapter, I want to tell you about two men famous to me. One of those was my grandfather, Walter Gisel. He was a man of character. He also took time to pour his wisdom into me. I would regularly see him at the kitchen table reading his Bible and doing his devotions. He would let me sit on his lap and participate if I wanted. My grandfather understood that he was an ambassador, not carrying his message but that of his God—and he carried that message wherever he went.

Another man of character was my uncle Dale Rowell, who worked every day to ensure his environment was ripe for his legacy to grow. My favorite story about Uncle Dale is that he would run alongside the sanitation workers and help them load garbage into the truck. He is the only person I've ever heard of doing that. Why did he do this, you may ask? Good question—and I once asked Uncle Dale the same thing. His response was, "I just want them to know they matter."

That is legacy...a deep understanding that people matter more than things, events, and discoveries. Yes, things, events, and discoveries are important and historic, but people are the essence—and reflection—of our legacy. And I hope I am doing a good job of growing the legacy of both my grandfather and my uncle through the environment they created.

13

FROM PEOPLE DEVELOPMENT
TO PERSONHOOD:
Your Lighthouse

Two radio operators, one of them aboard a U.S. Navy ship, had the following exchange:

Radio 1: Please divert your course fifteen degrees to the north to avoid a collision.

Radio 2: Recommend you divert YOUR course fifteen degrees.

Radio 1: This is the captain of a U.S. Navy ship. I say again, divert your course.

Radio 2: No, I say again, divert YOUR course.

Radio 1: This is an aircraft carrier of the U.S. Navy. We are a large warship. Divert your course now!

Radio 2: This is a lighthouse. Your call.[1]

Although this isn't a true story, it's a great story—especially for a Michigander.

Sharice and I finished raising our kids in Grand Haven, Michigan. There are numerous wonderful things about that state, but one of the best is Lake Michigan and the many lighthouses that dot the shoreline. Many people visit these lighthouses to take pictures, but the importance of lighthouses goes far beyond photography.

Lighthouses play a critical role for mariners, illuminating safe passage to destinations. The light emitted by a lighthouse glows faintly in the distance but grows brighter the closer a vessel is to the shoreline, thereby helping to orient mariners who, at times, become confused by the vastness of the sea or a large lake.

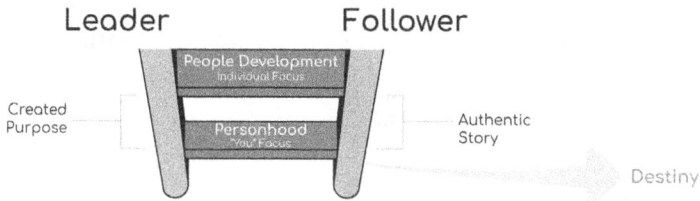

DESCENDING TO THE PERSONHOOD RUNG: LEADER'S ROLE

Understanding, and operating within, your created purpose is required for leaders to climb down from the *people development* rung.

Created purpose is your lighthouse. Created purpose is what has been guiding your safe passage toward your harbor, your destiny. Created purpose is understanding where, when, and how your unique gifting should be applied—thus maximizing the impact of your gifting.

Given that, why is created purpose at the bottom of the leadership ladder and not the top? Because often your created purpose, your lighthouse, doesn't come into clear view until after you have started your voyage. And this is the reason you must start your individual leadership journey—for until you start moving, you can neither turn your ship nor approach the shoreline of your destination.

>> CREATED PURPOSE IS ABOUT UNDERSTANDING WHERE, WHEN, AND HOW YOUR UNIQUE GIFTING SHOULD BE APPLIED—THUS MAXIMIZING THE IMPACT OF YOUR GIFTING.

For organizations, the created purpose is normally known from the outset, because most organizations are founded to solve a specific problem and/or to improve on something that already exists. However, as time passes, that purpose can fade from view, as the management demands of running the organization dominate its existence…and the organization neglects and can even forget its original purpose.

How does that happen? And how can an organization discover its purpose again? And how does an individual determine his/her purpose for the first time?

From Small Town to Small Ship

Perhaps the best way to answer that is to let you in on my journey and how I discovered my created purpose, my reason for existence.

I grew up in a tiny college town: no stoplights, a restaurant or two, one convenience store, and a handful of gas stations. I didn't have a clear direction of where my life was heading…but I found the United States Navy and its nuclear power program to be of interest. And fortunately, I was selected into that program. I guess being from a small town may have been why I was drawn to submarines —smaller vessels that have smaller crews than other nuclear-powered ships, such as aircraft carriers.

Prior to arriving on my first submarine, I made multiple assumptions—including one about leadership. I assumed if you were the Commanding Officer (CO) of a nearly $1 billion submarine, then you must be a good leader. I believed the military was a great-leader-generating machine.

That assumption was shattered when I had my first crisis of leadership on the boat, when my CO called me into his stateroom for the first time to scream at me. This became a daily practice…his way of "people development," I guess.

I remember wondering at the time if the CO's approach was poor leadership or if it was good leadership that I just didn't understand. If good leadership, then the military's view of (good) leadership seemed…flawed. If poor leadership, then I needed to determine what good leadership actually was.

I ultimately determined my CO wasn't exhibiting good leadership and that I needed to "find" an example of good leadership. At this time, I began to realize that my purpose in life was to fill leadership voids where I believed them to exist.

So, as a twenty-three-year-old Lieutenant Junior Grade with this purpose as my lighthouse, I set my voyage plan and began moving toward my destination. Again, movement is essential, because only after you get your ship moving can you turn it. If you wait to begin until the seas are calm and the fog is clear, you'll never arrive.

EMPLOYMENT TO DEPLOYMENT

Now, you might be thinking, "That's an interesting anecdote, Brian, but it doesn't apply to me because I didn't grow up in a small town or join the navy; nor do I consider my purpose to concern leadership." Thoughts along those lines are plausible reactions to a story about my created purpose, so let me shed light on the process of finding *yours*.

One part of the process is trying to connect what you get paid to do with what you enjoy doing. In other words, linking your employment to your deployment, joining a job to your purpose. Doing this is possible. First, you must believe you can connect the two (job and purpose). Then you need to look for ways to make this connection. Now, that connection may not be completely seamless at all times, but the connection should be evident for you—and even others—to realize that you are closing the gap between your employment and deployment. Let's take this a little deeper and examine three things that pertain to linking your employment to your deployment.

First, you need to understand what unique gifting and talents you possess.

Gifts are the raw materials given to you; things built into you when you were created. Gifts are given so they can be used for the benefit of others. Gifts tend to be intangible, not immediately (or always) visible; in fact, some say that gifts are "spiritual" in nature. For example, *administration* and *hospitality* are gifts. Being gifted in administration and hospitality doesn't mean others can't administrate well or be hospitable; rather being gifted in those areas means that you administrate in a more significant way than others and that your hospitality has a special warmth or appeal that others' doesn't. Unfortunately, gifts often remain dormant, like a present that remains wrapped, unopened. That is, we're cognizant that we have been given gifts, but we are often unsure what those specific gifts are because they often don't manifest themselves in physical form.

Conversely, talents are tangible, innate abilities that naturally allow us to perform certain tasks better than others. Talents tend to be something we use and that people readily recognize—like athleticism. I was not created with an abundance of athleticism, so I was regularly amazed by *athletes* who jetted by me in a marathon, even though they had trained very little as distance runners. Similarly, I was impressed by people who played golf only a handful of times a year yet could still beat me by ten strokes. Sometimes, we don't see our talents as *talents* because they come naturally to us; consequently, others often recognize our talents before we do. So that's one way to discover a talent—to listen to what others say we're good at doing.

Second, you must be willing to enhance those gifts/talents through developing skills. Skills are what you utilize to make your gifts more effective and talents more useable, resulting in you being the absolute best version of "you" possible. Discovering your gifts/talents and then enhancing them through skills development will move you closer to your deployment. You enhance your skills through training and practice. If you are a talented communicator, you can enhance that talent through formal communication training or by practicing your communication in front of a mirror.

And third, you must apply those skills effectively. How? By using those skills and monitoring the output, the impact of that application—in real life situations. Skills are the bridge between gifts/talents and impact. Your natural talent and created gifts are your potential but will not provide impact without development. I played football at a small college. I was not a talented football player; my potential was less than most others on the team. Yet I earned a significant amount of playing time—more time than several players who had more talent than me. How? I focused on honing my skills so that I could maximize the impact of my talent—whereas others (more talented) didn't work as hard on their skills, and hence the impact of their talent was negligible. You can't expect to improve at anything without effort, without working to enhance the gifts/talents you've been given.

READY, AIM, INQUIRE

A second, and perhaps more important, part of this process is asking yourself some pointed questions. Questions cause us to think, to look inside where our purpose resides—where our Creator placed it. Helpful questions toward discovering your purpose include:

- Is there a problem I can solve?
- Is there something I can do that might benefit others?
- Is there something others always ask me to do?
- What do other people think I am uniquely positioned to do?

Here are two examples of how these questions were answered in real life.

David and Lynn Clouse had a problem to solve in 1995. They had a ski cabin for rent in Colorado; however, there wasn't a good mechanism by which to inform the public that the cabin was for rent. Yes, the Internet existed then, but it didn't serve all the needs of society like it does today. David had a computer programming background, so he and Lynn started VRBO.com

(Vacation Rentals by Owner) for their personal benefit, to solve a problem they had as a couple. Their personal solution eventually resulted in an amazing tool for others, both property owners and vacationers.

Throughout my career, people have frequently asked me to speak to groups. On the one hand, I never thought these requests were anything unusual, assuming that many people were asked to do public speaking. On the other hand, I was often surprised by these requests, as I did not consider myself a master of the English language—as scoring a 450 out of 800 on the verbal part of the SAT confirmed! But as the requests continued to come in and as the results continued to be positive (people commented on my ability to speak and the impact my talks had on them), I slowly began to understand that public communication was a key part of my purpose. But please know that I never would have embraced my speaking skill as "purpose" without others first seeing and then confirming that skill.

REDUCED VISIBILITY DETAIL

Contrary to popular belief, submarines mimic other warships at times by operating on the surface. Of course, skimming across the surface is not a sub's preferred operating mode; the purpose of a submarine is to remain undetected, and a submarine operating on the surface is as visible as a tennis ball can floating in a bathtub. However, to arrive at a sub's destination, surface operations are required.

When our sub surfaced in foggy conditions, we would station a "reduced visibility detail," which equated to having more people on the bridge, sounding the sub's horn, and ensuring that all radar systems were functioning accurately. We maintained this detail until the fog cleared, and and the boat moved at a very slow, safe speed. Yet we never stopped going forward.

To descend to the *personhood* rung, you might have to deploy a similar detail. You might have to be patient, revisit your leadership journey, recall those critical moments in your life that have pointed you in a specific direction, and operate cautiously until the fog clears. But you can discover or reconnect with your purpose if you truly desire!

Purpose can be a difficult thing to determine because, like leadership, it doesn't feel very tangible. Attaining a solid understanding of our purpose requires (a) finding our gifts and talents, (b) developing the skills to enhance said gifts and talents, and (c) connecting those skills to what will produce the greatest impact, a lasting impact that lives beyond you. So even when you feel confined by the fog of life, keep moving—delivering your gifts to those around you, seeing your talent as unique, and developing skills to make your uniqueness uniquely better.

DESCENDING TO THE PERSONHOOD RUNG: FOLLOWER'S ROLE

Authentic storytelling—detailed in chapter 7—is located at the top of the ladder on the leader's side but at the bottom on the follower's side. In order to climb down to the *personhood* rung, the place where followers become fully connected to who they were created to become, followers need to begin the leadership function of finding and telling their stories—which will enable them to create their own leadership ladders to start climbing down.

Followers emerging from the *people development* rung have started to find their untapped potential and are delivering more of who they are into the organization. Followers begin doing these things as a result of people development—which concerns helping others to find their personal stories and to layer those stories into the organization's stories.

When followers are equipped and allowed to function in a way they are wired by the Creator, they will deliver more to any organization. They will perform at a level far above typical expectations. Just like a screwdriver is very effective at affixing a screw to wood but not nearly as effective at affixing a nail, people encouraged to deliver their potential into an organization will become very effective contributors when their work matches their design.

Operating in alignment with how they were designed helps followers to develop their story and prepares them to start authentic storytelling in the future—so that they, as future leaders, can climb down from *position* to *permission* and from *permission* to *production*. Of course, their climb down will eventually result in the formation of other leaders' ladders, and this constant cycle of more and more leaders climbing down leadership ladders is what changes our world and makes an impact beyond what we thought was possible.

FINAL THOUGHTS

Created purpose is the reason you are here and is the lighthouse that has been guiding your leadership journey. The final step in climbing down as a leader involves bringing that lighthouse into clear view and starting to see beyond it—to your destiny. As your purpose comes into clearer focus (or is reignited), followers will begin telling their own stories and starting their climb down with others.

Leaders producing other leaders should be our focus as leaders, because any leader who loses sight of this will likely plow and scatter too little seed, leaving limited growth opportunities for his/her legacy. The motive for this multiplication should not be "*my* legacy" but rather "my *legacy*." Note the difference. Multiplication isn't about "you"—how great you are or how many leaders are under your tutelage. Rather, multiplication is about "legacy"—passing forward the messages, character, ideas, and thinking that have allowed you to lead others effectively. Furthermore, recall that legacy grows after your departure (from a job, an organization, or a planet!); thus legacy can't be about you but rather the things that move on and live far beyond your presence. This perpetual motion of leaders multiplying leaders so that legacy moves beyond individuals' lives is what generates progress, leaving the next generation better than the previous one.

Our arrival point at the bottom of the leadership ladder is the starting point for our followers to begin descending down *their* leadership ladders. So without further ado, let's climb down to the final rung of the ladder in the next chapter.

14

PERSONHOOD RUNG:
Who Are You?

In the opening chorus from one of its 1978 hit songs, a rock and roll band called The Who asked a very important question—many, many (many!) times in a row.

Who are you? / Who, who, who, who? / Who are you? / Who, who, who, who? / Who are you? / Who, who, who, who? / Who are you? / Who, who, who, who?

I could answer that question with: ENTJ, Di, Ruby, and Red/Green/Orange.

Great…so what does that mean?

Those are my results from four different personality profiles: Myers-Briggs, DiSC, Effectiveness Dimensions, and Primary Colors Personality Test.

Okay…again…so what does that mean?

Well, according to the output of those profiles, that means I am driven, competitive, confident, look for the big picture, believe I can influence others, am willing to take some risk, and can be a "butthead" at times (as noted earlier—apparently, I really like that word!).

"Big deal," you might say about personality profiles, and I rather agree with that sentiment…except that those profiles do provide us a window into our default settings, the hardwiring that makes us go. But do those results fully define who we are? No, they only provide insight into how we would typically respond in a situation. Who I am—who you are—is our *personhood*, a word that means "the state or condition of being you," and the condition of "you" can be broken down into three main components: body, soul, and spirit.

PERSONHOOD RUNG LEADERSHIP

The term *personhood* is a compound word comprised of *person*, who you are, and *hood*, meaning a "condition or quality." Personhood, then, is the condition of being who you are or who you were created to be. Now, just what does this have to do with leadership?

On the personhood rung, people follow you because of *you*, because they have experienced your impact directly or indirectly. People follow you because they realize that your impact as a leader has allowed *their* impact as leaders to increase. Of course, having followers whom you haven't directly impacted can feel strange, but that is what happens when you create an environment for your legacy to grow—some of the seeds you scatter fall on people you don't know and never intended to influence.

Personhood leadership manifests itself when you function exactly as you were created to function, as envisioned by the Designer when He knitted you together. So let's dig deeper into what we mean by "person."

THREE IN ONE

We each were put together with three parts: a body, a soul, and a spirit. The body is the visible, tangible system that requires very little explanation; the soul is where your will, emotions, and decision-making capacity reside; and your spirit is what connects you to the Creator. From a very basic perspective, that's who you are. But examine each of these a bit more.

Your body has a main control system, a nervous system that is operated by a central computer: the brain. The brain is a complicated central processing unit (CPU) that not only controls physical functions but also processes data to create bundles of information that is filed away for later use. Specifically, the hippocampus, the seahorse-shaped part of the brain that resides behind the ears, is one part of the brain that organizes information in short-term and long-term memory.

Your soul is your center of reasoning, and the location of your will, emotions, and decision-making functions. The soul, sometimes called the mind, has two main parts, conscious and non-conscious. The conscious mind works when we are awake; it functions at a slower pace than the non-conscious mind. The non-conscious mind works 24/7/365 and at speeds up to seven times faster than the conscious mind.

Your spirit is what gives life and connects you to the Creator. Again, regardless of your belief system, someone or something had to set this entire cycle of existence into motion, and I'll continue to refer to that someone as the Creator. To help make the concept of *spirit* more tangible, let's turn to technology. My iPhone is useful only if it has life—battery life. That battery doesn't have a charge in-and-of-itself. Rather, that battery must receive a charge from a power outlet. So, the power outlet can be considered, in this example, as the life-giving "spirit." The phone's outer shell, screen, and battery are the "body." And the phone's programming/software is its "soul."

BE HAPPY YOU ARE NOT ME

We are different. Not just you and me, but also you and me and everyone. For instance, many people grow up wondering where they'll find their daily bread and nightly shelter. Others do not. But coming from different environments does not mean that one group is superior or inferior to another. Because our environments don't make us; we make our environments (as discussed in chapter 13).

We are similar. Not just you and me but also you and me and everyone, because we all have a body, a soul, and a spirit. We're all built out of the same materials and have memories and common speech patterns (even though we speak different languages).

Most people struggle more with their differences than with their similarities. Unfortunately, we tend to highlight our differences—body shapes, gifts and talents, skin colors, emotional responses, etc.—when, in fact, we have far more similarities. What would be better, in my opinion, is if we celebrated *both* similarities *and* differences. Let's be glad, for example, that men and women are different, and let's celebrate what makes us unique while also embracing the fact that we have significant similarities.

The world we live in tends to equate "different" with "bad," and that's...bad. Because what makes us different—our one-of-a-kind-ness—is the essence of personhood. Personhood is about you becoming who you were designed to be, who you were created to become, the original intent for you existing at this time in history.

And once you discover that original intent, that purpose, then exploit it. That's right: exploit it. In our culture, exploit often has a negative connotation, but the root of the word means "to accomplish; productive working." So, *exploitation*, in the context of your original intent, means to utilize your design, to productively accomplish your purpose.

GETTING TO THE BOTTOM OF IT

So how the heck do we discover who we were designed to become?

Well, I'd be the guru of all gurus if I had the answer to that question boiled down into one or two sentences.

Instead, the best I have to offer is this: Once you've climbed down the ladder and are looking toward the final rung, the *personhood* rung, you'll likely be close to finding your unique design, the intersection of your gifts and purpose. Admittedly, that answer pertains more to *when* you discover personhood than to *how*.

143

And speaking of "when," am I stating that you must be old and gray to reach the *personhood* rung? Not necessarily. But you can't reach it until you have climbed down the other rungs of the ladder. In other words, (a) you must have effectively articulated an authentic story that (b) has facilitated inspired action in you and others (c) wherein your proven character has been displayed for others and then—and only then—your quest for personhood can commence fully.

On the leadership ladder, the *personhood* rung is unique in that, unlike the other rungs, you might not have personal contact with the individuals who have followed you to this place on your leadership journey. In other words, people who follow you because of personhood may not have a direct connection to you; they may only know you through what you've written, what others have said and written about you, or what others have experienced in following you. In other words, as your legacy grows, you may gain followers that you didn't directly impact but rather who were impacted by the power of your personhood, your legacy.

>> OUR ENVIRONMENTS DON'T MAKE US; WE MAKE OUR ENVIRONMENTS.

The influence inherent in personhood begins with discovering the intersection of your gifts and purpose and accelerates as your legacy grows over time. In other words, as people replicate your message, values, character, etc., others notice and start this replication. And what was once two people influenced by your personhood becomes four, and four becomes sixteen, and sixteen becomes sixty-four. That replication process will lead people back to the source, and thus your personhood becomes more evident and real—who you were created to be is on display, and others see who you are as someone they want to be.

PERSONHOOD PEOPLE

As we stated earlier, Jesus had a core group of mentees, followers (a) whom He spent time developing and (b) who then replicated in their followers what they learned from Him. Jesus' time on earth was more than 2,000 years ago, but the replication process he began has remained so strong that today we still try and emulate His behavior and His leadership. Jesus exemplifies personhood—people follow Him today because of who He was and what He represented.

Of the numerous modern-day examples of personhood, Martin Luther King, Jr. is a prominent one. Many people alive today personally interacted with Dr. King during his life, and those people continue to carry forward his character and his inside-out thinking that all people are made in the image of God. However, Dr. King's influence also continues today through thousands of people who were *not* alive when he lived but who nonetheless follow him because of who Dr. King was and what he represented.

Regarding a personal example, one of my gifts is communication—specifically, communicating ideas in a way that connects with others. My purpose is to help people find the keys to unlock their leadership potential so that they can find meaning and purpose in all areas of their life. When I was a vice president for a power services company, I spent time climbing down my leadership ladder, looking to develop people along the way. However, there was no way I could have a personal interaction with all the people because of the enormous size of the company. Did that stop me from trying to reach the *personhood* rung? No. Did I reach that rung with followers I didn't know? Yes. How do I know that? In my current job of training and developing leaders, I've run into several people from my former company who've said that they didn't know me but appreciated what I meant to the organization and to them. That is a small example of personhood.

Personhood Rung Outcomes

Ah, summer vacation. During the school year, kids long for the chance to load up the car with their siblings, drive for days with dad singing, stop to eat fast food every 4.39 hours, and then come home.

Um, not exactly. Kids want to go somewhere. Adults want to go somewhere! Hence people don't simply pile into the car to drive for days without a destination in mind.

What about your car, your life? Is there a clear destination ahead? (Death doesn't count, because we are all headed there.) Your destination is what you were created for, the place where your impact and influence are maximized. Just as you plan a family vacation starting with the end in mind, your life's destination needs to be well planned. After all, the outcome of leading on the *personhood* rung is arriving at your destination—your destiny!

And when you arrive at your destiny, others benefit. They see how their piece of life's puzzle, like yours, is necessary for the entire picture to be completed. They witness the value in pouring out what they have for the benefit of others. Personhood is where followers "leave the nest" and fly on their own—finding their own stories, wrestling with and embracing their authenticity, and refining their own storytelling. Personhood compels followers to begin climbing down their own ladders and to lead within their own stories by using their gifts...gaining followers as they descend.

Defining Destiny

To you, *destiny* may sound mysterious, religious, utopian, and a waste of time. However, upon examining the word origin, destiny simply means "to stand firm or to establish." I interpret *standing firm*, *being established* not to mean that you are at the end of your life but rather to mean that you have finally found that intersection of gifts and purpose. Let me try to paint a picture of destiny for you.

In chapter 13, I noted that created purpose is your lighthouse. Created purpose is what has been guiding your safe passage toward your destination. Your purpose—this lighthouse—is a grounded, immovable structure that gives light to your life's path. You might not realize your purpose yet, but it is nonetheless fixed, created within you.

Destiny is the port or harbor that is "home" to the maximum impact you can deliver as an individual. Think about a commercial shipping vessel; it was built to transport cargo, and its destiny is to arrive at the harbor where that cargo is delivered for maximum utilization. The same applies to our lives: Our destiny is the harbor, the location where the "cargo" that is our gifts and talents is delivered so that cargo can achieve maximum utilization. Taking this view allows us to understand that destiny is not some abstract, metaphysical condition that is unattainable but instead is a place in life where we realize a significant impact.

> DESTINY IS THE PORT OR HARBOR THAT IS "HOME" TO THE MAXIMUM IMPACT YOU CAN DELIVER AS AN INDIVIDUAL.

Given that, here's a critical question: Do you know the destination for your life, or is your life just a ship sailing around without a port to deliver its gifts and talents?

I could leave you hanging here, left to think that finding your destiny *might* be possible but is probably unlikely. Or, I could state something that might be a little obvious but nonetheless true...and that is this: The best chance you have to find your destiny is to get your ship moving.

I've never seen or heard of a ship reaching its destination without ever leaving port, yet many of us take that approach. We believe that our current port, the place we presently find ourselves, is where our ship will remain; thus we're convinced that dreaming about something bigger equates to expending brain cells that would be better used doing something else. If that's you—if you feel glued to the shoreline—start your engines, cast off your lines, and get underway, even if you can't clearly see the destination. As long as you continue to deliver your gifts while looking for where *best* to deliver them, your ship will get closer to the harbor that is your destiny. Is there some risk involved? Of course, but risk and reward go hand-in-hand. But then, with nothing ventured, nothing is gained, so get moving on your (ad)venture!

FINAL THOUGHTS

Who Are You? was a popular song in 1978 and also a question we should continue to ask ourselves. Personhood is what makes you uniquely you, and personhood is found where your gifts/talents, what makes you uniquely different, align with your purpose, your original intent.

On the *personhood* rung of the leadership ladder, destiny is realized when you arrive at the destination for which you were created. "Arriving" doesn't mean you've reached the end of your life; instead, arriving means you've reached a new beginning, the place where your life is in full bloom, the harbor where your unique cargo is delivered for the benefit of others.

Personhood is at the bottom of the leadership ladder for a reason: You gain an understanding of who you are as you move down the ladder. As you descend (defining and refining your stories, learning how to tell them as you embrace and prove who you are), if you are looking for your purpose throughout your climb, you will find it. Being at the bottom of the leadership ladder means you are at a place where you are pouring out all of your uniqueness for the benefit of others, footing ladders for others to climb, continuing to plow and scatter for the benefit of legacy, and increasing your value as your visibility continues to decrease.

15

THEORY TO PRACTICE

The nuclear navy has some strict inspection criteria. During a typical inspection, there are exams, training observations, evaluated maintenance activities, and records reviews. One of the items reviewed is the Theory to Practice exercises. Theory to Practice is what the name implies: an idea is birthed, a hypothesis regarding an outcome is created, and an experiment is conducted. The goal of the experiment is to obtain actual data and compare it to the theoretical data from the hypothesis. In this way, Theory to Practice exercises are great tools for enhancing knowledge, understanding, and application.

Knowledge, understanding, and application are vital for leading well. Knowledge involves becoming aware of something new, such as a fact, an opinion, a detail, a process, etc.; to me, *knowledge* and *information* are synonymous. Understanding goes deeper, beyond knowledge, however, because understanding involves comprehending knowledge at a level sufficient for an individual to teach or to communicate regarding knowledge effectively to another. Knowledge, then, is the student, while understanding is the teacher. Application involves *action*—the act of putting to work the knowledge and understanding a specific situation.

If we, as leaders, *know* and *understand* but don't *apply*, we're working with only two legs of a three-legged stool—we're ineffective. Effective leaders move from understanding to application, putting into practice what they understand about good leadership and observing if what happens (the outcomes of their practice) matches their hypothesis about what *should* happen. Specific to what we have been discussing within these pages, leaders apply the leadership ladder and then observe if they obtain followers, make history, leave a legacy, and arrive at their destiny.

The previous fourteen chapters of this book dealt with the first two legs of the stool—knowledge and understanding. These are always the first two legs that make possible the third leg, application, which is the focus of this chapter. Herein, my goal is to give you a taste of how the leadership ladder works within a few different settings—so that the application of the leadership ladder to your situation becomes a little clearer.

>> EFFECTIVE LEADERS MOVE FROM UNDERSTANDING TO APPLICATION, PUTTING INTO PRACTICE WHAT THEY UNDERSTAND ABOUT GOOD LEADERSHIP AND OBSERVING IF WHAT HAPPENS (THE OUTCOMES OF THEIR PRACTICE) MATCHES THEIR HYPOTHESIS ABOUT WHAT *SHOULD* HAPPEN.

ONE LEADER'S LADDER

Jesus is a polarizing figure, but this is not new news (1 Peter 2:7-8). So instead of debating who Jesus was or is, let's simply examine His approach to leadership. Did this approach follow the leadership ladder, or did Jesus utilize a different method?

As background, Jesus was about thirty years of age when He started his public ministry. Jesus was preceded in that work by John the Baptist, who set the stage for Jesus, but Jesus nonetheless started as…a positional leader (*everyone* starts on that rung).

"Follow me, and I will make you fishers of men" (Matt. 4:19) was the story Jesus told while walking along the Sea of Galilee. Remember, an authentic story is a picture of the future that is

(a) better than the present reality and (b) is communicated with originality. So, let's vet Jesus' statements through our authentic story filter. Jesus was inviting people to join Him. In this case, He invited fishermen. They were small-business owners and expert anglers, but what was this claim about catching men? That claim was a unique spin on their occupation—but did it create a picture of the future that was better than their present reality communicated with originality? Well, *"immediately, they left their nets and followed him"* (Matt. 4:20). So, yes, the fishermen believed in the future Jesus' story offered them, and they permitted Him to lead.

After Jesus assembled His team of followers, He had to take actions that were inspired by His story. What actions are inspired by a vision to fish for men? Here is what the eyewitnesses tell us: *"When Jesus went ashore, He saw a large crowd, and He felt compassion for them because they were like sheep without a shepherd; and He began to teach them many things."* (Mark 6:34)… *"Getting up, He went from there to the region of Judea and beyond the Jordan; crowds gathered around Him again, and, according to His custom, He once more began to teach them"* (Mark 10:1). Teaching was one of Jesus' inspired actions; in the four Gospels, there are more than thirty-four instances of large crowds following Jesus as He taught. *"When He went ashore, He saw a large crowd, and felt compassion for them and healed their sick"* (Matt. 14:14). *"And the blind and the lame came to Him in the temple, and He healed them"* (Matt. 21:14). Healing was another type of inspired action that was connected to Jesus' story of fishing for men.

Inspired actions alone don't move one from the *permission* to the *production* rung, however. The empowerment box must be offered by the leader and accepted by the follower.

"And He called the twelve together and gave them power and authority over all the demons and to heal diseases. And He sent them out to proclaim the kingdom of God and to perform healing" (Luke 9:1-2). In that passage, you see the word "authority," which establishes the boundaries of the empowerment box, but what about knowledge, skills, and attitude? These twelve guys

had been witness to all the teaching Jesus had done with large crowds, and the twelve were also recipients of the small-group training they received as they traveled with Jesus. *"Jesus went out, along with His disciples, to the villages of Caesarea Philippi; and on the way He questioned His disciples, saying to them, 'Who do people say that I am?' They told Him, saying, John the Baptist; and others say Elijah; but others, one of the prophets. And He continued by questioning them, 'But who do you say that I am?' Peter answered and said to Him, 'You are the Christ.' And He warned them to tell no one about Him. And He began to teach them that the Son of Man must suffer many things and be rejected by the elders and the chief priests and the scribes, and be killed, and after three days rise again. And He was stating the matter plainly. And Peter took Him aside and began to rebuke Him. But turning around and seeing His disciples, He rebuked Peter and said, 'Get behind Me, Satan; for you are not setting your mind on God's interests, but man's'"* (Mark 8:27-30). Here, we see Jesus working through knowledge toward understanding with his twelve closest friends. Additionally, we see Jesus working with Peter on the application of said knowledge and understanding; Peter incorrectly rebukes Jesus, and Jesus subsequently corrects Peter's action.

Jesus had created a clear empowerment box bound by the authority to cast out unclean spirits and to cure sickness. (Note that clarity creates a strong, healthy empowerment box.) Did the twelve accept the empowerment offered? Indeed, they did. *"Departing, they began going throughout the villages, preaching the gospel and healing everywhere"* (Luke 9:6).

At this stage in His ministry, Jesus was now on the *production* rung, having told an authentic story, having gained followers' trust, having taken inspired actions, and having empowered His followers. Did Jesus stop there? No, He continued to prove his character: *"… One who has been tempted in all things as we are, yet without sin"* (Hebrews 4:15). He was compassionate (Matt. 15:32), humble (John 13:12), forgiving (Matt. 6:14), patient (Matt. 26:38-45), and gentle (Matt. 11:28). This is just a short list of character traits Jesus displayed.

Did His followers want to be developed? *"It happened that while Jesus was praying in a certain place, after He had finished, one of His disciples said to Him, Lord, teach us to pray just as John also taught his disciples"* (Luke 11:1).... *"I brought him to Your disciples, and they could not cure him. And Jesus answered and said, 'You unbelieving and perverted generation, how long shall I be with you? How long shall I put up with you? Bring him here to Me.' And Jesus rebuked him, and the demon came out of him, and the boy was cured at once. Then the disciples came to Jesus privately and said, 'Why could we not drive it out?'"* (Matt. 17:16-19)

When people want to be developed, they start asking questions to understand how the leader functions. Why? People want to be developed by a leader who they aspire to emulate. The disciples wanted to be more like Jesus, indicating their desire to be developed by Him. Eventually, they replicated Jesus, functioned similarly by healing the sick (Acts 3:7-8), casting out demons (Mark 6:13), and preaching His kingdom (Acts 3:12-26).

People development is about replicating the leader—becoming similar to the leader in message, action, and function. That said, please remember that replication isn't best displayed by the *quality* of the performance but rather by the *desire* to speak and act like the leader. The disciples, for instance, did not do things as well as Jesus did. However, their actions did certainly remind people of Jesus, and that is replication. The result of this replication was an environment for Jesus' legacy to be created, and today, people still aspire to be like Jesus, growing His legacy even larger.

Finally, did Jesus make it to the *personhood* rung? Did He find His created purpose?

"I have manifested Your name to the men whom You gave Me out of the world; they were Yours, and You gave them to Me, and they have kept Your word. Now they have come to know that everything You have given Me is from You; for the words which You gave Me I have given to them; and they received them and truly understood that I came forth from You, and they believed that You sent Me" (John 17:6-9).

And did He help the disciples find their story?

"But Peter, taking his stand with the eleven, raised his voice and declared to them: Men of Judea and all you who live in Jerusalem, let this be known to you and give heed to my words" (Acts 4.14).... *"And with many other words [Peter] solemnly testified and kept on exhorting them, saying, 'Be saved from this perverse generation!' So then, those who had received his word were baptized; and that day there were added about three thousand souls. They were continually devoting themselves to the apostles' teaching and to fellowship, to the breaking of bread and to prayer. Everyone kept feeling a sense of awe; and many wonders and signs were taking place through the apostles"* (Acts 4:40-43).

So, did Jesus reach his destiny?

"I glorified [God] on the earth, having accomplished the work which [God has] given Me to do" (John 17:4).

You might think that all I am doing here is trying to fit what Jesus did into the *Climbing Down* model to justify the model. Please test the model for yourself, read the four Gospels, and look at how Jesus the leader functioned. I welcome your feedback after you perform this exercise.

FROM THE HEART

I normally approach things headfirst; that is, I lead with my head. My wife, Sharice, often says, "Don't talk *at* me; have a conversation *with* me." She encourages me to speak from my heart because when she sees my heart, she hears my message. I'm not sure if the previous chapters have felt like I've been writing with my head, with my heart, or both; but for the next few paragraphs, I'll be communicating directly from the heart.

Sharice and I went to high school together. We dated briefly during that time, but that shared experience impacted us differently. And this is not surprising—life frequently works in such a way that two people experience a similar event, but what's recorded in their minds is dissimilar.

Sharice believed we would get back together one day, but I didn't. She was correct, but we each had to grow through some experiences first. Sharice had a beautiful baby boy after graduating from high school, and her pregnancy drew her towards faith. I had grown up with faith but was struggling with the necessity of it. You might say our trajectories were moving in different directions when our paths crossed again—Sharice's trajectory upward and mine downward. The good news about trajectories, though, is they can be changed.

We married in 1988. I then joined the navy, and we made the first of what will be nineteen moves at the writing of this book. I said the good news about trajectories is they can change, but getting a new job, moving to a new geographic location, and/ or adding members to the family (more kids) may not change a trajectory; none of those things changed mine. Well, …what did, then? My trajectory changed for two reasons: Sharice's unwavering faith and a big stick upside my head! Sharice never lost hope—hope in the source of her faith. She believed in God's promises and believed they would be fulfilled. Sharice's hope allowed God to grab the nearest spiritual two-by-four and apply it squarely across the back of my head, stopping my current trajectory and starting to turn me back towards Him.

The result of this reversed trajectory was that our marriage started becoming what we believed it could be—two people becoming one, not in body but in dreams and desires. And that's what our story is about, connecting our dreams and desires to deliver a bigger impact than we could separately. Now, that doesn't mean our gifts are the same. Sharice is creative, a builder, and able to enhance the beauty of what already exists. I'm better with a pencil than with a hammer, able to simplify difficult concepts and connect with people through communication and story-telling. I prefer cooking to cutting lumber for a project. Sharice would rather spend time in the garage or with a paintbrush. She watches HGTV; I prefer ESPN. How can we be so different yet have such a great marriage, make history, leave a legacy, and reach our destination?

All this starts by agreeing upon a shared purpose and then writing a story—creating a pathway—that takes us to the destination established by our shared purpose. How do we, as separate beings, maintain our uniqueness, our authenticity in a shared environment? We write our individual chapters, thus maintaining our own identity within the pages of the shared story. We find and enhance our gifts through skill development, looking for ways (note the plural!) to deliver those gifts.

In marriage, people sometimes see themselves as winners and losers; either the husband or the wife "wins" by pursuing his/her dream, and the other spouse loses. Reducing marriage to winners and losers eventually results in either the male or female being the most important—instead of both being "most important." Do not dismiss your competitive nature, but *do* stop competing against one another; instead, channel that competitive drive together—strive *with* not *against* one another—to keep moving toward the destination, adding chapters to your story as you fight through the challenges of life.

BOARDROOM AND BEDROOM

What if we looked at marriage through the lenses of leadership and management? What if we took the principles that work in the boardroom and applied them in the bedroom? Okay, I don't literally mean in the bedroom, but I certainly am advocating that we apply leadership and management principles to our marriages and families. In my house, such an application might look like this.

- Brian cooking and Sharice fixing things around the house

- Sharice paying the bills and Brian handling the investments

- Brian talking to a stranger about leadership and Sharice rearranging the photo wall at her in-law's house

- Sharice making our house a home and Brian holding her ladder

- Brian watching the boy's hockey practice and Sharice working at the children's school

- Sharice leading a women's Bible study and Brian leading a men's ministry

- Brian's career resulting in another relocation and Sharice building a box maze for the kids

- Sharice repeatedly describing our destination and Brian paving a new road to get there

This is a brief list of common life activities. What might not be common is the balance of those activities within a marriage. Shouldn't the woman cook things and the man fix things? Perhaps—but not necessarily. In our marriage, Sharice cooked for many years, and I hung a few ceiling fans and light fixtures, yes. A strong relationship, though, is not about "should and should not" but rather about balance, understanding that leadership and management functions pertain to life's activities. Remember, leading is about authentic storytelling, inspired actions, character, and purpose. Management is about completing tasks, installing processes, and taking actions that move us in the desired direction. Making our house into a home is a leadership function; steadying the stepladder is a management function. Paying the bills is a management function; financial investing is a leadership function. Watching the boys' hockey practice is management, and helping to shape the kids' school curriculum is leadership. Keeping the destination in front of us is leadership, and paving a new road to get there is management.

Now, I'm not suggesting that Sharice and I have always understood these activities as "leadership" or "management." We initially did not have the knowledge or the perspective to view activities in that way. However, we did instinctively know that connecting our gifts to our marriage activities would create the best outcome. Does that mean you should only do the things that you like or can do well? Of course not. But neither am I suggesting that you ignore your gifts because of some "wrong" thinking that says, "Only the man should do this (e.g. fixing), and only the woman should do that (e.g. cooking)." Connecting your gifts to the leadership and management activities in your marriage will change your marriage for the better.

Sharice and I have both written chapters in our authentic stories that have resulted in us trusting one another. We have taken actions inspired by those stories and empowered each other. Our character has been proven, and we are better together, helping to develop each other's whole person: spirit, soul, and body. Finally, we know we have a created purpose. Our created purpose is often the combination of many little things that together create a major impact. For example, created purpose for Sharice is cutting a friend's hair, helping decorate a house, making a Halloween costume, and serving at the food pantry. For me, created purpose is telling a stranger that he/she is uniquely gifted and purposed, communicating a difficult concept to a friend, and encouraging a co-worker.

The above is not meant to be "look how great Brian and Sharice are;" rather it is a transparent way for me to tell you that I know you can find balance in your life because *we* found balance in our lives. I believe the best way to find such balance is to continually seek to discover your gift, see what story that gift points toward, combine your efforts with others, and know that both the journey and destination matter. My desire, *our* desire, is that this book has allowed you to step out of your current reality into a better future—that through reading these chapters, your head, if hung low in defeat, has raised up and your future is now visible. Please know that whoever you are, you are uniquely gifted and uniquely purposed.

FINAL THOUGHTS

Sisyphus was the king of Corinth in Greek mythology. His punishment for some bad behavior was to roll an immense boulder up a hill, only to watch it roll back down—and he had to repeat that process forever. (Not fun.)

Applying the leadership information and knowledge you've learned can make you feel like Sisyphus; you may feel "punished" as you try things that don't seem to have any impact, seeing more mistakes than successes. However, knowledge and understanding, when applied effectively, can move boulders up—and over—mountains.

This book can be the key to unlocking the leadership potential you have inside and have always had inside, resulting in deeper, broader influence within your personal and organizational spheres. Remember, your leadership potential is much more about who you are than about what you do. What you do is your history, and we all have a history…as represented by dates on our resume or tombstone that encompass the events of our lives. We can be remembered by those events and slowly fade from others' minds as time marches on, or we can be ever-present as our legacy grows through the people we've helped develop during our lifetime.

We have that choice.

After all, life is about choices. I've presented many of those choices in these pages.

- The choice between (a) thinking in a "status quo" way or (b) renewing your mind, changing the way you think to enable your leadership.

- The choice between (a) leaving your intrinsic leadership capacity dormant or (b) growing your leadership through *Climbing Down*.

- The choice between (a) over-managing yourself and others or (b) balancing your leadership and management to achieve results beyond what you've envisioned.

- The choice between (a) running alone or (b) empowering others to run alongside you.

- The choice between (a) discovering your purpose now or (b) wishing, at the end of your life, you had done so.

I told a story in chapter 5 about my brother attempting to climb up a ladder while lugging a pack of roof shingles. The point of that story really does summarize *Climbing Down*: Why struggle towards the top of the ladder carrying a heavy load when you can climb down, lightening your load as you descend, impacting others you encounter on the climb and eventually reaching your destination? You do have a choice. And I hope this book has persuaded—and equipped—you to...

KEEP CLIMBING DOWN!

AUTHOR'S NOTE

My name is Brian Roth, and my story is to help people discover the keys to unlock their leadership potential so they can find purpose and meaning in all areas of their lives. How did I discover that story? I joined the navy after college in hopes of using my physics degree. That resulted in being assigned to the nuclear navy and submarines. I spent twenty-two years in the navy, twelve on active duty and ten in the reserves. Growing up in a small town, I assumed that all people at the top echelons of the military were great leaders. That isn't what I found, so I continued my search for great leadership.

I remember saying once that if it works at work, it should work at home. Those around me thought I was joking, but in this case, I was very serious. That saying allowed me to work through leadership at home with my wife and three kids. Could I find great leadership and apply it within the walls of my home? Leading one's children is a strange concept for many who believe all that is required of a parent is to manage, to serve as an authority for children. My wife, Sharice, and I desired to be more than just "authority figures" for our children, however. We worked to understand how to balance leadership and management in our marriage and parenting. Searching for this balance was the first milestone along my leadership development journey.

The quest for the correct view of leadership continued as I gained influence as a submarine officer in the navy, first as a junior officer and then as the Engineer onboard USS *Oklahoma City* (SSN723). The pace of my growth as a leader was rapid;

most of my department changed out during a shipyard period, and I was required to provide new team members with leadership through authentic storytelling that guided inspired actions. Simultaneously, I was endeavoring to earn trust and to empower team members as co-laborers, working through the many challenges of shipyard life to re-establish operational status for the sub.

Eventually, I chose to leave active duty in the navy but continued leading in the reserves, earning my joint forces certification and supporting one of the major combatant commands, Pacific Command (PACOM). In this role, I not only led junior sailors, soldiers, airman, and Marines but also was able to observe the leadership of generals and admirals in both real and simulated scenarios. This experience was another significant milestone along my leadership journey.

During my time in the reserves, we settled our family in Michigan and found a local church. There, I was afforded opportunities to lead the men's ministry for several years and to serve as a congregational elder. These roles allowed me to apply good leadership principles within the testing ground of a non-profit organization. There might not be a more challenging leadership setting than within non-profit organizations because the primary interaction is with volunteers. But once again, good leadership principles found a home, even in this volunteer-centric environment.

The most recent milestone on my leadership journey has been in the business world, working first as a plant manager at a power plant and eventually moving to the corporate office as vice president of operation and maintenance services (VP O&M Services). At the power plant, we had a very small staff relative to the megawatts of electricity we produced, so balancing leadership and management in the plant was critical. We were incredibly successful at this balance; consequently, I received an offer to transition to the corporate office.

My phone rang one day while on vacation in Daytona Beach. The president of the company was calling, so naturally, I felt obligated to answer. He asked if I would be willing to assist him, as he was going to remove the current VP of operations due to the poor execution of the business. I said that I would be happy to help, but also asked him why he couldn't simply offer me the job. "Why would I do that?" he asked. Certainly, a legitimate question. My response stunned him briefly, as I said, "If I can't make a noticeable difference in the business within six months, I will quit—no strings attached." Of course, I'm certainly not recommending that everyone take this approach, but our president was impressed with (or at least curious about) my offer, so he gave me the job...that I held for more than six years! Apparently, he saw a noticeable difference. Throughout those six years, our company doubled the number of contracts, increased our revenue by 80%, and raised our profit by 150%. How did we do that? By balancing our leadership and management and by applying sound leadership principles, many contained in *Climbing Down*.

I am thankful for my journey and believe in my ability to convey a message that others can understand and apply...thanks, in part, to my education. No, I did not study rhetoric or composition in college. My undergraduate degree is in physics, and I have a master's in acoustics. What do these have to do with leadership? Not much, directly speaking. But these highly technical degrees have benefitted me as a leadership communicator by requiring me to understand how to take difficult topics and articulate them in a manner that facilitates understanding, regardless of the background of the listener. And in addition to my education, I have had experience as a communicator, as I've been afforded the opportunity to speak at many different events in my roles as the president of a local Gideon's chapter, at a regional Promise Keepers conference, at city council meetings as a plant manager, and to conferences as the VP of O&M Services.

My understanding of leadership and the ability to convey a message is why I recently started my leadership coaching and consulting company. Pursuing this business required me to leave my position as VP O&M Services. My company, Employment 2 Deployment, was created (a) to unlock the leadership potential that remains dormant in many people and organizations and

(b) to connect those people and organizations to a purpose—to move people from merely making a living to making a difference. I believe the message of *Climbing Down* will connect differently than most leadership books because the efficacy of its principles has been demonstrated in various places such as the U.S. Navy, my family, a non-profit organization (church), and in the business world.

More information is available at www.employment2deploy ment.com.

MORE ABOUT *CLIMBING DOWN*

Hello. Thank you for reading *Climbing Down*. I hope you found the materials touchable and tangible and that your leadership is better because of it. I thought explaining how I arrived at *Climbing Down* might be useful.

A LITTLE ABOUT ME

First, you need to know that I was a sarcastic and cynical teenager. Yes, that's true, but not unusual; perhaps you can relate? (And perhaps you feel that "sarcastic" and "cynical" are redundant to the term *teenager*!)

While in college, I joined the United States Navy. Why? Because I was a great patriot committed to my country? No. I joined the navy because I was committed to me. The navy paid me while I finished college; the navy allowed me to escape the small town where I grew up; and the navy had something that interested me: nuclear submarines.

I learned a lot—I changed a lot—between beginning my naval career as a "me-first" kid and ending it as a commander. (Funny thing, that relationship between learning and change!) My time in the navy broadened my perspective on everyday life and exemplary leadership tremendously.

Specific to the latter, the "leadership" of some Commanding Officers during my early years in the navy puzzled me. They did not inspire; they lacked a vision, and they seldom gave me a reason to follow them—other than because of their position as captain.

165

How could that be? How could the person responsible for a $1 billion naval submarine, with 130 officers and crew capable of inflicting significant damage in an engagement, be an average leader? Or worse, a non-leader?

This line of thinking launched me on a quest for answers—to better understand leadership in order to apply it more effectively. I have been on that quest for more than thirty years, and that quest has become my purpose: to help people unlock their leadership potential.

A LITTLE ABOUT WISDOM

You probably noticed the influence of several people explicit on the pages of this book.

Dr. Myles Munroe, Dr. John Maxwell, and Simon Sinek are among those who have influenced my thinking on leadership. These men have written books and shared principles that inspired me to work not only toward gaining knowledge about how to lead more effectively but also toward striving for a deeper understanding of leadership principles.

To what end was this inspiration? Was it simply for the sake of accumulating knowledge and understanding so that I could become the smartest person in a room full of smart people?

No. This inspiration was bigger than that.

These thinkers inspired me to become effective in applying the knowledge and understanding I'd gained by studying them and other persons of influence. They inspired me to be wise.

We often refer to people as "wise" if they possess much knowledge and understanding. In the Bible, King Solomon was one of those people. What made Solomon wise? Yes, he possessed much knowledge and understanding, but, more significantly, he could apply said knowledge and understanding more effectively than others. Wisdom, then, involves action—the application of knowledge and understanding. And without action/application, knowledge is just knowledge, and understanding is just understanding.

An example from the navy can help to further distinguish knowledge from understanding from wisdom. In a submarine, before one is permitted to operate equipment, one must become certified, a process that involves three stages. The first stage is gaining knowledge of the system—learning about the equipment inherent to the system and how to properly operate it. One gains this knowledge by reading books that explain the equipment and by observing people who are certified to use the equipment. The second stage is completing a verbal check-off. This check-off provides the opportunity for one to "teach" the knowledge gained to a qualified individual to demonstrate a sufficient comprehension of that knowledge. The third stage is operating the equipment—physically moving switches, opening and closing valves, and properly communicating those functions to others. The desired outcome is achieved by properly operating the equipment, representing the application of knowledge and understanding.

A LITTLE ABOUT MY INTENTION

Leaders who produce make history, leaders who develop leave a legacy, but leaders who descend…have a chance to reach their destiny, their created purpose. So, this book is written for leaders—meaning this book is written for everyone. That's right. For you, me, Sharice, Steve, Dawn, Jessica, and Jim. We all are leaders because when the Creator formed humans, He placed within each of us the capacity to lead and to manage.

Since the Creator created us to lead, why don't we? The answer, in large part, is because we don't know how to activate our leadership potential—we lack the keys to unlock our leadership potential. Thus, such potential lies dormant, which results in our lives having less impact than they otherwise could.

Enter *Climbing Down: How Leaders Descend Toward Their Destiny*. This book:

- clarifies the difference between leadership and management;

- provides a model to help unlock your leadership potential; and

- equips you to apply that leadership model in tangible, meaningful ways.

We live in a world of immediate gratification, from fast food to fast money to fast travel. This immediacy mentality often fosters the temptation to focus on processes at the expense of principles. That is, we can become so keen on getting to C that we "do" A and B, in the equation $A + B = C$, without ever considering if A and B are healthy or appropriate. Applying $A + B$ without understanding the principle(s) behind them will achieve C, but maybe not the desired C.

Within the context of real life, we often admire a successful company or parents whose kids are "great." There is certainly nothing wrong with esteeming companies and families, but we make a mistake if we emulate their activities (processes) while missing their approach (philosophy). Yes, focusing on process instead of philosophy tends to be the easier route, because, typically, processes are tangible, measurable, and replicative, whereas philosophies are…not. However, such a focus can be short-sighted, leaving us with no explanation when "it worked for them so it will work for us" doesn't actually work for us. And we become frustrated, after a time, because our businesses or our children don't seem to be growing in the areas we had anticipated.

But we could prevent a great deal of this frustration, I contend, if, instead of mimicking what a business or family does, we discern why they function as they do. That is, we should first learn their principles and then apply those principles within our unique business or familial context.

That's wisdom…applying knowledge and understanding with specificity to your set of circumstances and objectives.

Regarding such application, I learned a valuable lesson from my father. He taught college physics for thirty-three years. During this time, he would spend, in my opinion, an inordinate amount of time studying in preparation to teach. I struggled with why, after teaching the same course year after year, he continued to study. He was obviously a smart guy, so there had to be a reason.

When I was a teenager, instead of merely asking him why he studied so much, I (being the sarcastic, cynical type, as previously noted) said to him something like, "The last time I looked, physics has not changed much over the years, yet you continue to study it." I knew he was book smart, but I was banking on my street smarts getting the best of him; I was sure that my comment would flummox my pocket-protector-wearing father.

Well, as shocking as this is, I was wrong.

My dad's response revealed that he had wisdom, not simply knowledge and understanding. He said, "If I don't understand a given topic from a 360-degree perspective, I might not be able to apply that knowledge in a way that will allow me to reach all the students, because everyone learns differently." In other words, if he couldn't (a) apply his understanding of physics to a specific student's learning style or (b) apply his knowledge in multiple directions, then his effectiveness as an instructor would suffer. (Don't you hate when your parents come up with that one response that stops you in your tracks?)

My dad's answer certainly forced me to stop and think—and his answer has stayed with me for more than thirty years. Hence, I am compelled to ask, "Are you making a conscious effort to apply your knowledge and understanding to your specific situations?"

A LITTLE ABOUT WHAT THIS BOOK CAN'T DO FOR YOU

This book will not make you a great leader. There are two primary reasons for this.

First, great leaders activate their leadership capacity by connecting with a purpose, a destiny, a reason for existing—and then daily take steps to move closer to actualizing that destiny. How you lead best is how you lead best; in other words, lead "in your area of gifting." And while this book can show you the importance of purpose, it cannot *give* you your purpose.

Second, leadership requires practice. Although this book will help you see what true leadership looks like in different contexts, practicing leadership—doing it—is required to maximize your ability to lead in your specific situation and within your specific area of gifting. Likewise, professional athletes or musicians practice incessantly, as they are continually preparing themselves to perform better next time than last time.

Related to this point, I recall hearing John Maxwell tell a story about a guy who had read one of his books and said, "Where were you twenty years ago? I could have used this information then." To that comment, Maxwell replied, "You wouldn't have wanted to hear what I had to say twenty years ago." Maxwell's point was that twenty years ago his leadership skills and philosophies were not practiced, honed enough to be of use to others.

Now, you may be thinking, "No matter my purpose or how hard I practice, this book won't make me a great leader or any kind of leader…because I was not born to lead." I disagree. I believe everyone is born with the capacity to lead, but many people struggle to activate their leadership gift (and if you don't believe that you possess the necessary DNA to lead, your leadership will forever lie dormant).

Let me provide additional commentary to that claim.

In addition to studying great leaders, I also spend time studying the Bible, which provides both a foundation that has shaped my leadership beliefs and a filter through which I process all my decisions. The Bible teaches that God created humanity and assigned us a purpose. Part of that purpose is to have dominion over the earth God created (Genesis 1:26). Dominion contains the ideas of both leadership and management. Therefore, I believe all humans are wired to lead and to manage; however, most do not activate their leadership DNA—either because they don't know how or because they've been told, by someone who doesn't understand leadership, that they will never be a leader.

The design of this book is to help activate your leadership gift. You are wired to lead and to manage. My desire is to help you along your journey, and my prayer is that God would bless you along the way!

END NOTES

Chapter 1

1. Sinek, Simon, *Start with Why: How Great Leaders Inspire Everyone to Take Action.* New York, NY: Penguin Group, 2009, Print

Chapter 2

1. Maxwell, John, *21 Irrefutable Laws of Leadership, 2nd Edition.* Nashville, TN: Thomas Nelson, 2007, Print

2. Drucker, Peter, *Management: Tasks, Responsibilities, Practices.* New York, NY: Collins Business, 2008, Print

3. Munroe, Myles, *Becoming a Leader*, Lanham Seabrook, MD: Pneuma Life Publishing, 1999, Print

Chapter 3

1. Bon Jovi, John. "Bad Medicine." New Jersey, Mercury Records, 1988.

2. Strong, James, *The Exhaustive Concordance of the Bible*, Nashville, TN: Thomas Nelson, 1990, Print

Chapter 4

1. Sinek, Simon, *Start with Why: How Great Leaders Inspire Everyone to Take Action.* New York, NY: Penguin Group, 2009, Print

Chapter 7

1. King, Martin Luther, Jr. "Address Delivered at the March on Washington for Jobs and Freedom," Washington, D.C., August 28, 1963, Web, kinginstitute.stanford.edu/king-papers/documents/i-have-dream-address-delivered-march-washington-jobs-and-freedom

Chapter 8

1. Lencioni, Patrick *The Advantage, 1st Edition*. San Francisco, CA: Jossey-Bass, 2012, Print

Chapter 9

1. King, Martin Luther, Jr. "Address Delivered at the March on Washington for Jobs and Freedom," Washington, D.C., August 28, 1963, Web, kinginstitute.stanford.edu/king-papers/documents/i-have-dream-address-delivered-march-washington-jobs-and-freedom

Chapter 10

1. Maxwell, John, *5 Levels of Leadership, 2nd Edition*. New York, NY: Center Street Hachette Book Group, 2011, Print

Chapter 11

1. "Stress Testing - Investopedia." *https://www.investopedia.com/terms/s/stresstesting.asp* Web. 02 Dec. 2018

2. @RSherman_25. "Peyton is the classiest person/player I have ever met! I could learn so much from him! Thank you for being a great Competitor and person." *Twitter*, 03 Feb 2014, 12:40 a.m., https://twitter.com/RSherman_25/status/430214142398849024?ref_src=twsrc%5Etfw%7Ctwcamp%5Etweetembed%7Ctwterm%5E430214142398849024&ref_url=https%3A%2F%2Fftw.usatoday.com%2F2014%2F02%2Frichard-sherman-peyton-manning-super-bowl

Chapter 12

1. Means, Stephen. "Urban Meyer retiring, Ryan Day taking over Ohio State football program: Press conference transcript of everything they said." *Cleveland.com*, 04 Dec 2018, cleveland.com/osu/2018/12/urban-meyer-retiring-ryan-day-taking-over-ohio-state-football-program-press-conference-transcript-of-everything-they-said.html

2. Bender, Bill, "What is Urban Meyer's legacy at Ohio State? Depends on whom you ask." *MSN.com*, Microsoft News, 04 Dec 2018, msn.com/en-us/sports/ncaafb/what-is-urban-meyers-legacy-at-ohio-state-depends-on-whom-you-ask/ar-BBQviQm

3. Ellis, Linda, "The Dash," Southwestern Inspire Kindness, LLC, 1996-2019, thedashpoem.com

4. Collins, Jim, *Good to Great, 1st Edition*. New York, NY: Harper Business, 2001, Print

Chapter 13

1. Addis, David. "Standoff: Navy Says No Lighthouse—No Comment." Virginian-Pilot. 14 March 1996 (p. A1).